Animal Hero Kids

Voices for the Voiceless

by Susan Hargreaves,
founder of Animal Hero Kids

Saoirse, Super Animal Hero Story at the end of this book.

Published in the United States of America
by Animal Hero Kids animalherokids.org

Susan Hargreaves, Founder
Animal Hero Kids
1225 NW 21st Street, Suite 503
Stuart, FL 34994   USA
susanh@animalherokids.org
animalherokids.org
tel. (561) 575-5517

ISBN 978-0-615-99522-9
Printed and bound in the United States of America
1 2 3 4 5 15 16 17 18 19

Founder of Animal Hero Kids and Author: Susan Hargreaves
Contributing Authors: Sir Paul McCartney, Thomas Ponce, Simone Reyes, JP Dyben, Ingrid Newkirk
Editor: Tanjah Estelle Karvonen, Valence Translations & Editorial valenceeditorial@gmail.com
Reviewers: Prad Basu, Carol Keyworth, Alexi Howk, Marianne Guerra, Micheline Karvonen, Guy Stanford
Art Direction, Layout, & Design: Cynthia Cake, Toronto
Illustrations: Leslie Walters, Artworks, Toronto http://lesliewalters.wix.com/artworks,
Marco Morales, Keenie Valega, Richard WhiteCloud, Sam Hussein, Zach Teper, Robin Bodiford,
"Be Kind to All Animals" Poster Contest Winners
Photo Research and Content Research: Susan Hargreaves, Margie Pacher
Cover photo: Katie and Colby Procyk
Cover Design: Cynthia Cake, Toronto

Catherine Violet Hubbard, Animal Hero Kid

Six year-old animal lover Catherine Violet Hubbard was kind. She would tell other creatures, "tell your friends that I am kind" so they would know they could come visit in safety. Catherine Violet, an Animal Hero Kid— her love for animals will live on in the 34 acre animal sanctuary being built to honor her dream. Catherine Violet was killed in a mass shooting at Sandy Hook Elementary School on December 14th, 2012.

Voices for the Voiceless Poem

I am the Voice of the Voiceless
Through me the dumb shall speak
Till the world's deaf ear be made to hear
The wrongs of the wordless weak.
Oh shame on the mothers of mortals
Who do not stoop to teach
The sorrow that lies in dear dumb eyes
The sorrow that has no speech.
From street, from cage, from kennel
From stable and from zoo
The wall of my tortured kin proclaims the sin
Of the mighty against the frail.
But I am my brother's keeper
And I shall fight their fight
And speak the word for beast and bird
Till the world shall set things right.

Ella Wheeler Wilcox, 1910

Table of Contents

Section 3: Wildlife Animal Hero Kids

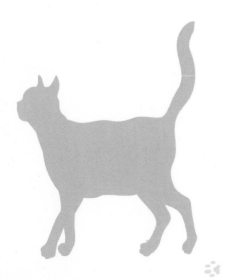

Introduction

You are holding in your hands a key to helping animals in need. By helping other beings, we create a better society and thereby help ourselves as well. This book is a celebration of kind actions inspired by compassion and implemented with positive practicality. It is an empowering guidebook to creating heroes for animals!

I have been a humane educator and animal activist all my adult life. In my 32 years of presenting humane education programs in schools across North America, I have had the privilege of meeting children and teenagers who are voices for animals in need — young people who speak out against injustice and animal cruelty. They know it is wrong to harm others and are courageous enough to say so. When young people learn about the plight of homeless companion animals, the suffering of factory-farmed animals, and the misery of captive circus animals, their strong sense of empathy and justice compel them to act!

I began recognizing Animal Hero Kids by presenting awards to them in front of their peers in schools and at public events over 20 years ago.

Animal heroes can be all ages!

Aaliyanah was 6 years old when she was recognized with an Animal Hero Award. After speaking to city commissioners, she was able to help get the electro-shock prods and bull hooks used on elephants banned. The ban effectively stopped circuses with performing animals from coming to Miramar, Florida.

There is the group of young people (Teakahlah, 7 years old, Aaron, 12, and Denise, 13) who saved hundreds of sea turtle hatchlings from certain death on Fort Lauderdale beaches through their volunteer work with Sea Turtle Oversight Protection (STOP).

Dominic, at the age of 9, became Animal Hero Kids' Crew President and organized a monthly protest outside of the Miami Seaquarium where orcas, dolphins, and seals are jailed.

Thirteen-year-old Kelsey was host of her own vegetarian cooking show, where she met former NFL player, Ricky Williams, at one of the Annual Animal Hero Kids Awards.

Teens from Urban Tails, a closed group home on county jail grounds, who adopt out abused dogs, after helping them to trust again, were among the attendees from around the U.S. who were at the awards.

What does Animal Hero Kids do?

The mission of Animal Hero Kids is to foster empathy and kindness in children and young people by encouraging and recognizing compassionate and courageous acts that help all species of animals. We also offer complimentary, interactive, humane education programs highlighting stories of the rescue and aid of animals in need.

November is World Animal Hero Kids Month. One hundred and sixty organizations have signed up to encourage and recognize Animal Hero Kids locally. One of the Animal Hero Kids award categories is the Russell Simmons Creative Animal Hero Kids Award for an individual or group under the age of 19 who creates a song, a dance, a spoken word performance, piece of art or a video that inspires others to help animals. The Sir Paul McCartney Young Veg Advocate Award is for an individual or group under the age of 19 who promotes kind food choices.

Reaching 30,000 children and adults each year with direct, humane education programs with the help of the Animal Hero Kids volunteers, on a very small budget, is a challenge. Yet, Animal Hero Kids are on the rise everywhere, around the globe, across North America, in your town, in your school, and perhaps even in your home!

"You can judge a man's true character by the way he treats his fellow animals."

Sir Paul McCartney

Insurance for the future!

I remain hopeful that more people are making kind, informed choices. I am continuously encouraged and impressed by the actions and voices of Animal Hero Kids. You will be too when you read about the young people and the animals they help to live free from harm.

 Please visit our website at www.animalherokids.org for updated stories.

You may wish to nominate an Animal Hero kid or teen, collaborate, sponsor, donate or volunteer with our all-volunteer 501c3 non-profit charity. You could also participate in World Animal Hero Kids Month activities.

What follows are the inspiring stories of young people who have helped all sorts of animals, in all sorts of situations... and who are indeed animal heroes.

Susan Hargreaves

Author's Note about Animal Categories

I feel that all domestic animals, whether they live on farms or in houses, have the capacity to be companions to us, human animals, and to each other. I am not the only one who feels this way, ask George Clooney about Max, his cherished companion pig. I have separated this book into three sections, heroes to Companion Animals, Farm Animals, and Wild Animals. It is purely with the intention of making this book easy to read and to help all species of animals.

Thank you to all of the parents and teachers who support their children and teens in realizing their dreams and wishes to help animals in need.

Animal Hero Kids Mega Kind to All Award

December 2, 2013
Los Angeles, California

Animal Hero Kids is proud to recognize

Ellen DeGeneres

For embodying the spirit of compassion through her kind support of others,
whether two-legged or four,
and for making a lasting, positive difference for humans, animals, and the environment.

*Congratulations to my fellow award winners.
Animal Hero Kids Rock…it doesn't matter how young or
old you are, the good news is you can help animals in need.*
-Sir Paul McCartney

*Encouraging and Recognizing Animal
Hero Kids for 32 Years*
Animal Hero Kids

Chapter 1

Companion Animals Need You!

Animal Hero Kids Inc. gave a special award (the Mega Kind to All Award) to a great adult role model in Los Angeles, on December 2nd, 2013. The award was for a person who is known for being very kind to animals. The students at the Art Institute of Los Angeles have created beautiful works of art for each and every award we presented.

Here is the Mega Kind to All Award. Read it and you will find out who the recipient is.

Companion Animal Hero Kids

Animal Hero Kids

© Tina K Valant

Dominic is one very active Animal Hero Kids Co-President. He is pictured here with his dog, Luna, who was rescued.

Here is Animal Hero Kids' Canada president Jasmine, with Kelli, a rescued chick.

Arielle is our eloquent teen Animal Hero Kids Co-President, pictured here with Joseph Turkey at CJ Acres Sanctuary.

Aaliyanah is our talented Animal Hero Kids Co-President, who frequently speaks up for animals at protests.

Standing: Michelle Cintron, Humane Educator/Program Coordinator; Ibrahim Morales, 11;
Carla Sofía Cortés, 10 (Holding the horse photo); Alessandra Morales, 11;
Bottom Row: Andrés Cortés, 12; Camila Cortés, 7; José Cortés, 5; Mom and Dad;
Yari Albelo - tutor; Carlos Cortés - tutor

A Picture is Worth a 1,000 Words

Puerto Rican Animal Hero Kids Rock...

There is a small island called Culebra close to Puerto Rico. The children on this island may not have a lot, but they do have a lot of heart. They decided to make a difference for the animals on the island who were not cared for, animals that may be homeless or perhaps neglected or abused. The Federación Protectora de Animales de Puerto Rico and the Fundación para el Capital Social gave the students cameras to take home from school to capture images showing how other animals in the community live. The observations the students made with their photos and quotes opened the eyes of others in the community to how other animals were being treated. Their photos, accompanied by their written thoughts or wishes, are powerful.

2013 Animal Hero Kids Awards in LA

You can see these photos for yourself here and periodically throughout the book.

Thanks to the determination of local animal advocate Michelle Cintron and the kindness of some of the kids' parents, the kids traveled to the annual awards. It was so great to meet some of these kind kids when they received their Animal Hero Kids Award (2013 Los Angeles Animal Hero Kids Awards).

Did You Know?

- 🐾 Three to five thousand puppies and kittens are born every hour in the United States.

- 🐾 There are 45 cats and 15 dogs who come into this world, for every person born.

- 🐾 Animal shelters and pounds take in approximately 27 million lost or abandoned dogs and cats every year. 20 million of them never find a home.

My dream is that the animals have good parents and take care of them and give them baths and a lot of food. The street animals could be adopted. I want that the people could do the best to make them to be happier. If I had the power I wouldn't let the animals feel abandoned and sadness. I would like that all the abandoned animals could be like my dog he always loves to play he is very happy and he obeys. I give him a lot of love.

ADARA 12

PHOTO VOICE
Culebra 2013

FUNDACIÓN CAPITAL

In the same corner of the globe
is a teen super hero who
has swooped down to care for
homeless dogs and cats.

Natalia, Teen Hero Aids Puerto Rico's Homeless Cats and Dogs in Crisis

"It is estimated that more than 1,000,000 stray dogs roam the streets of Puerto Rico, and it's anyone's guess as to how many stray and feral cats are on the island. The animals are everywhere and many are hungry, and in need of medical care. It's hard to look at them day in and day out. Many people look away and pretend not to see", wrote Joy Sarnelli Carson, the Executive Director of Pets Alive in Puerto Rico when she nominated 14-year-old Natalia Maisonet for an Animal Hero Teen Award.

Natalia's eyes and heart were opened to the plight of animals in Puerto Rico when she saw that unwanted and abandoned animals were everywhere. Soon Natalia was rescuing animals,. Her first rescue was a two-day old kitten. Natalia bottle fed her and cared for her lovingly, and

9

when the kitten was ready, Natalia found her a permanent home. She did the same with a tiny puppy she found on the street. Natalia realized she wanted to do more to help animals and reach more people, so she founded "Alley Cats & Dogs Rescue."

Since then, Natalia has rescued, rehabilitated, and found responsible, loving homes for 60 cats and dogs – and she spayed/neutered 11 of those animals before having them adopted out.

Some of Natalia's rescues have had special needs, and she nursed them patiently – like the tiny pup, born in the jungle, whose leg was severed when it became entangled in a vine. Many bottle-baby kittens and puppies need round-the-clock care.

In addition to her rescue work, Natalia cares for three community cat colonies (a total of about 40 cats). She feeds them daily, she vaccinates them, she treats them for common skin ailments, and, if they get sick, she takes them to the veterinarian. Natalia's latest project is to raise enough money to spay/neuter all the cats in her colonies, and so far, she has spayed/neutered 17 of them.

Natalia gets support from her mother when needed, but mostly she raises the money herself to fund the TNR project, to care for the colonies, and to rescue dogs and cats in need. She does this by making and selling chocolate lollipops and cupcakes, and by volunteering at the local veterinarian's office in return for reduced rates. Her "Alley Cats & Dog Rescue" Facebook page has more than 1,300 followers.

Natalia also speaks at schools to educate others about the life-saving importance of adopting, spaying and neutering companion animals.

I was so glad to meet Natalia and her mom in person at an animal care conference. Go to animalherokids.org for an update on Natalia's 2014 nomination result.

QUIZ QUESTION

Circle which options below are part of the solution to the problem of homeless animals.

a) Pet stores who breed or buy from breeders while animals are dying in shelters and at animal rescues.

b) Shelters looking for homes for the animals that exist right now, and spay or neuter all cats and dogs who enter their doors.

c) Exotic animal or wildlife sellers who breed or steal animals from their natural home; hermit crabs, exotic birds, baby squirrels, pythons, and other types of wildlife.

d) A person who advocates to adopt, spay or neuter in order to prevent companion animal suffering by educating their friends, family, and teachers.

🐾 **What can you discover in your community with a camera about how animals are treated?**

🐾 **Are there famous photos you can think of that helped create positive change in history?**

🐾 **If the subjects in your photos could talk, what would they say?**

🐾 **Are there community centers or libraries or schools that would consider having a photo display of how other animals are treated in your community?**

🐾 **What would you call the photo display?**

🐾 **Can you think of a way you can help your local shelter by taking photos of animals?**

Former NFL star, Ricky Williams, and a group of Animal Hero Kids and awards

Chapter 2

Liberty City, Miami, and the Accidental Animal Hero Kids Crew

Computers and social media have brought us the information age. This has become a great tool for animals in need by educating using powerful images, and encouraging kinder choices. We can then make better informed decisions about what to wear, the type of entertainment to see, why and where to adopt companion animals, and what to eat. So much information is now on the computer, which means I often sit at the computer... usually bleary eyed at

Khareem, with a rescue dog named Honey, one of the Animal Hero Kids who saved Winnie

night. I do have a tendency to fall asleep at the keyboard, my nose landing, somewhere around the letter "G".

It was on one such evening, I saw a plea for veterinary costs to be paid for a little 7 month old rescued black puppy. She had suffered such severe injuries that her back leg would have to be amputated. Studying the e-mail, I learned this dog was rescued by a group of 8 children ranging in age from 8 to 13 years old. I had to investigate...

It was a late Sunday afternoon in Miami's Liberty City neighborhood as friends played: Jakara, 8; Ladena, 9; Rantrell, 12; and Janika, Paulemy, Dominique, Khareem and Julian, who were all 13 years old.

They saw a small black dog running away from someone who was chasing her. They watched, horrified, and saw the little black puppy being pushed down the sewer grate. Paulemy ran to get Tia Williams, the local "dog" lady, while everyone else waited by the ominously quiet drain. They were able to pry the storm drain lid off and Tia went down into the drain to retrieve a very silent, wet, and severely injured puppy.

The dog's leg was crushed to the extent that it had to be amputated. Tia and the kids could not afford the vet costs.

Khareem wrote in the Animal Hero Kids newsletter...

"Grateful Paws Rescue in Fort Lauderdale was the only rescue that would help us afford veterinary care, so we started volunteering with them. We found a great home for Winnie but decided there were lots more animals out there that needed our help."

This incident started most of the rescuers on the road to volunteering to help animals in need.

These Animal Hero Kids were featured in many newspaper articles and their story was covered by many TV news stations.

I gave an assembly award presentation to Miami-Dade students at both Leonore B. Smith Elementary and Allapattah Middle School. All of the local print and TV media came out to film the lucky, now three-legged, pup named Winnie and her rescuers.

Here's a quote from the NBC news report: *"I'm surprised she's running with three legs," said Julian, one of the students who helped rescue the 8-month-old pup. "I'm just glad she got a home."*

Today, Winnie is very happy in her forever home. Winnie and her rescuers attended one of our annual award celebrations. The little puppy had turned into a healthy and robust dog compared to that little defenseless pup I had met a few years before. Ricky Williams, the former NFL star, congratulated the kids at an annual awards event, whose quick, brave actions saved this pup's life.

Activity Ideas!

QUIZ QUESTION

❖ Can you find out what the laws are in your State about harming animals?

❖ Who would you call if you saw an animal in trouble?

❖ What if a kitten were stuck in a tree? Who would you call?

❖ Do the laws in your community need to be changed? In Section 3, read about 13 year old Thomas Ponce's lobbying work to change laws to protect more animals. Intentional cruelty to animals is a felony in many areas.

❖ Research the local police and humane society phone numbers to find out who you would call in your own community to report animal abuse.

❖ Discuss why the children in this rescue story went to a trusted adult for help.

"The golden rule is you treat people how you want to be treated and that includes animals, if you treat animals and people kindly, you will be treated kindly and you will have a happy life."

-NFL star, Ricky Williams

Kitten Rescue

Dominic, Co-President of Animal Hero Kids, traveled to congratulate an Animal Hero Kids Role Model. Errand Frazier heard purring coming from inside the body of his pick-up truck. He could not reach or see where the purring was coming from. He sprang into action and, with his tools, sliced a hole in the body of his truck. Look at the photo below to see who he found!

Errand received the Animal Hero Kids Role Model award. Kitten is now happy in her forever home and is called Angel.

*Animal Hero Kids'
Co-President, Dominic,
meets kitten rescuer,
Errand Frazier.*

21

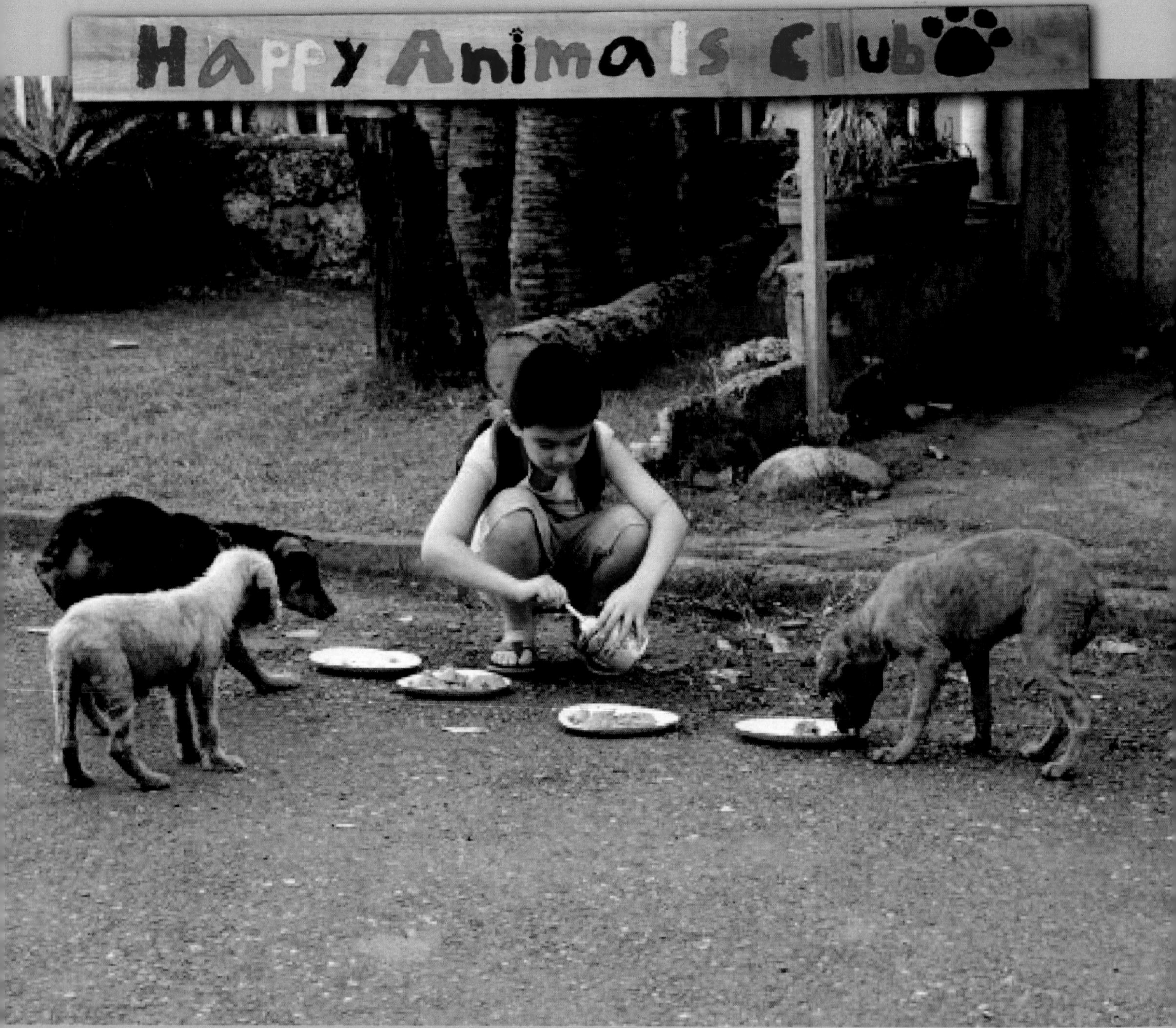
Happy Animals Club

The Happy Animals Club
in the Philippines

Ken is a 2014 Animal Hero Kid nominee who lives in the Philippines. Here's his story, in his own words, from his website...

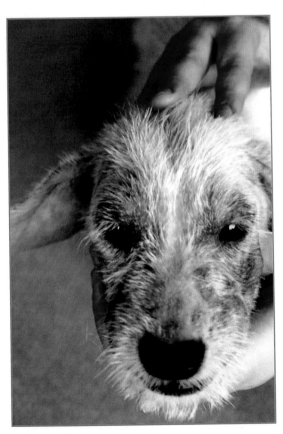

White Puppy with mange (before)

"I love animals. I have one rescue dog and two rescue cats. Ever since I can remember I wanted to open an animal shelter to help the stray dogs and cats on the streets. My dad told me it would take a lot of money and 20 years for me to get an animal shelter. He said only grownups can raise enough money to start an animal shelter. But in February of 2014 pictures of me feeding dogs on the street were passed around on the Internet. Here are those pictures.

Some very kind people who saw these pictures donated money to help me care for the dogs. We got enough money to get the dogs I was feeding off the street, to feed them high-quality canned food, and to provide them with veterinary care.

They gained a LOT of weight, their open wounds healed, and their fur grew back. They also learned not to be scared of humans.

Here's how they look after two months of care at Happy Animals Club. Their names are Blackie, Brownie, and White Puppy and they will be ready for adoption very soon!

The Happy Animals Club's main goal will be to rescue dogs from the city pound. In an article dated March 20, 2014, the official at the pound said most dogs are put down because only about 20%-30% of owners claim their dogs, and no animal welfare organization is doing something about it.

White Puppy all better! (after)

Using the funds raised from the happyanimalsclub.org website, on May 1, 2014, I leased a 1000 square meter (10 000 square feet) lot for one year. I bought two little bamboo huts called bahay kubo as shelter for the dogs when it rains. Everyone expected me to put the dogs in cages but the dogs won't be happy if they are locked up in cages. The huts cost 16,000 pesos each or about $370. The roof is made from native grasses. There is enough room for many dogs in each hut. I can't wait to see dogs in the huts. I know they will be very happy.

We need to have a system for finding the dogs good homes when they are ready. This is a big challenge because in the Philippines most people want pure breed dogs. They don't like mutts, even though mutts are just as smart, just as loyal, and just as loving.

Ken has gained the support of his community. Adults are pitching in to assist with permitting, construction, and advocating for the success of the Happy Animals Club Shelter.

 Check out Ken's progress at happyanimalsclub.org and watch for updates at animalherokids.org.

- In the Philippines, some people eat dog meat, an indigenous practice that also can be traced back to early religious rituals. The majority of Filipinos, however, no longer consume dog meat.

- In the capital city of Manila, Metro Manila Commission Ordinance 82-05 specifically prohibits the killing and selling of dogs for food. The Philippine Animal Welfare Act of 1998 prohibits the killing of many animals (for human consumption), including all dogs.

- In India, there is a whole segment of the population that considers the cow holy and believes that cows should not be eaten.

- 🐾 Find the Philippines on a world map.

- 🐾 Research articles you can find on the Internet with respect to the treatment of companion animals in the Philippines and any animal protection groups there and their campaigns.

- 🐾 Discuss how the cultural climate of a country such as the Philippines or Puerto Rico can influence people's treatment of (companion) animals and how it takes a lot of courage to stand up for animals and be an animal hero when you might have less support in your community.

- 🐾 Imagine if a Martian came to Earth and they had never heard of any animals being eaten.

Chapter 3
Animal Friends

Lovey, Animal Hero Kids' Most Loving Volunteer

Animal Hero Kids is an all-volunteer organization and one of our biggest supporters is, without a doubt, Lovey Hargreaves. Lovey was a stray found wandering in Wellington, Florida. She had ear infections, was very thin, and her coat was matted and dirty. The Palm Beach County Animal Control is an open admission shelter which means they cannot say, "we are full, we cannot take any more dogs and cats", which results in many animals being

Important lessons in kindness

KIT BRADSHAW • kit.bradshaw@scripps.com

...reaves hol...ovey next to the truck that she has for her humane efforts. It features a photo of Lovey and other animals on the ...ac...

t...ns resident helps children learn to be kind to animals

...ORAL
kit.bradshaw

It took ch...experiences — from horrendous conditi... at a poultry farm...re her...a worked or s...g abou... ...d...d by...used...

shown extraordinary kindness to animals, such as the youngsters in Liberty City who rescued a puppy stuffed into a drainage ditch and left to die, who received the award last year.

...w...there is a new opportunity

teaching humane education program to foster compassion toward others, I've never had an opportunity like this, and I'm thrilled to be able to offer this scholarship," Hargreaves said.

so they can put themselves in the animal's place."

Hargreaves said this education fosters compassion and empathy in children that will stay with them all their lives. "These are the building blocks of being kind...

euthanized. Nationally, approximately 4 to 5 million companion animals are killed each year in shelters. When I visited the shelter, it was very hard for me to pick just one dog, there were so many dogs and cats I knew were scheduled to be killed. My purpose was to adopt to save a life. Lovey joined our family of 6 rescued canines and felines. One of her dog brothers, Connor, weighs 110 pounds and his head is bigger than Lovey's whole body! He is so gentle with her.

Here is Lovey, Connor, and our Animal Hero Kids Co-Presidents Dominic, Arielle, and Aaliyanah at the beach.

Animal Hero Kids' direct humane education presentations promoting being kind to all animals reach 30,000 children and adults each year. If a program or award presentation is not too loud and I know Lovey will be comfortable, Lovey will come to the schools with me. If I am holding her, Lovey is fearless and feels secure. She needs to know I am not going to leave her behind and she will not be lost again. Whenever I walk into a school room with her, all eyes are on Lovey. A reporter visited the house and the photo she took of Lovey ended up on the front page of the newspaper. In the photo, Lovey is looking at an enlarged photo of herself on the side of the Compassion Cruiser car, the car I use to visit schools and spread the message of kindness to all animals.

Did You Know?

🐾 It is proven that a dog or a cat companion can calm and soothe their human guardians.

🐾 Dogs are pack animals and their human family is part of their pack. It is unnatural to keep a dog away from his or her human family. Dogs will suffer if kept in backyards all the time, instead of in the house.

🐾 Dogs can hear 10 times louder than humans and at higher frequencies than we can. This means that if something is loud for us, it may damage the hearing or cause discomfort or distress for your canine friend.

Activity Ideas!

* Find out if there are humane education presentations offered in your local area.

* How would you create your own presentation for your own school, scout troop, or club to educate about how to help other animals?

* Are there ways you can get the word out about the animals up for adoption in your community?

* If you have a class or a group, ask students to think of four companion animal issues to discuss. Then choose issues where there may be split opinions, for example, keeping dogs outside in dog houses versus letting them live in the house with the family. Ask students to think about what constitutes companion animal neglect, companion animal abuse, and what actions against companion animals should be punished by the law. Once students have found four good issues, break the class into two debating teams. Go over with students the basic rules for a classroom debate. Allow each side a certain number of minutes to present their argument and/or to refute the other side's argument.

Book Buddies
Reading with Companions

I love it when kids help animals and
animals help kids – at the same time!
This story is a prime example.

The people who work at the Animal Rescue League of Berks County in Pennsylvania know from first-hand experience, that cats are the number one abandoned animal in the United States. The cats in their shelter can get very lonely waiting for someone to adopt them. Kristy, a staff member, asked her 10 year old son, Sean, if he would read to the cats. The goal was to improve his reading skills and to comfort the cats. This brilliant idea grew into the "Book Buddies" program. Each child reads a total of five books to the cats. The touching photos of the first and second graders from the local school reading to the cats went viral on the Internet and were seen around the world. People were inspired to adopt the cats and donations increased at the shelter.

The photo on the front cover of this book is of Colby Procyk reading to a cat who was adopted after the photo was taken. Colby says "I feel awesome helping the cats and all animals. I really like to help them feel loved until they can find their forever home."

Did You Know?

- Cats living in Florida and other hot climates have more than one time of the year they have babies.

- The Egyptians worshiped the magical powers of cats.

- Cats can see 10 times better in the dark than the most advanced night vision glasses created by humans.

- Cats clean themselves and do not need humans to bathe them.

Activity Ideas!

- Can you start your own "Book Buddies" program by talking to your English teacher at school and people from your local shelter?

- Can you write down the titles of five books that you think a cat would appreciate?

- Can you write a story about a cat that ends up in a shelter from the cat's point of view?

- Can you find out if there are free or low cost spay or neuter programs in your neighborhood?

- You don't need to have a drama club or drama program at your school to brainstorm real-life situations you have experienced, heard about, or read about companion animals in need of help. Parents, teachers or students can search for newspaper articles to stimulate brainstorming, or create a few examples of your own to get started. Teachers can ask students to imagine 8 to 10 situations where companion animals are in need of our help. Have them break into groups of 3 or 4 and choose one situation to work on. Students can then prepare a short skit to act out and explain their situation to their classmates. Leave a brief question and answer period at the end of each skit.

Chapter 4

1,000's of Kids and Teens Uniting Against Animal Cruelty

When Lou Wegner learned about the huge number of dogs and cats being euthanized in shelters, he decided to do something about it. Lou created Kids Against Animal Cruelty with the mission to use social media networking to find homes for animals in shelters that are in danger of being killed. Five years later, Kids Against Animal Cruelty's Facebook page has almost 23,000

likes, with 50,000 supporters, 19 chapters in the United States and 3 global chapters, in Greece, Nepal, and Belgium. Thanks to members and partner coalitions thousands of animals have been saved from death in shelters. Here's what Lou says:

"Our mission is to spread the word to adopt from shelters, to spay or neuter your pet, and to please be pet responsible. We are Animal Rights Knights fighting for the rights of all animals. Please be kind to people, animals, and our planet. Through our sites on Facebook, we inform our members and guests about the plight of animals all over the United States and in several foreign countries, who are in desperate need of rescue. Networking greatly increases the chances for animals on death row that, in most cases, have about a week to live. By spreading the news, we have successfully rescued and placed thousands of animals in permanent, safe, and loving homes."

**Kids Against Animal Cruelty has a chapter in Greece.
Penelope Pirri is the chapter president. Here's her message:**

"The Animal Hero Tip I would like to give to other children is to Adopt/Love/Protect/Spay-Neuter which is written on our KAAC flag and I think it is the most inclusive message. If we spay or neuter our pets, we will not have so many strays. Also, if we adopt a shelter pet we save two lives: the one adopted and the one that will take its place and if we love and protect them the world will be a better place."

At the Los Angeles Animal Hero Kids Awards, Lou received the Ricky Williams Animal Hero Teen Award for saving thousands of companion animals scheduled to be euthanized in shelters.

The award was presented by the previous years' Ricky Williams Animal Hero Teen Award recipient, Juliette West. Her story is featured in Section 3.

Booboo Stewart, a wolf character from the *Twilight Saga*, also presented the award.

Did You Know?

- ❖ If there were 8 dogs in every home in the United States, there still would not be enough homes for all the stray dogs that exist right now.

- ❖ Dogs and cats are less likely to get cancer if they are spayed or neutered.

"The only creatures that are evolved enough to convey pure love are dogs and infants."

~ Johnny Depp

Activity Ideas!

- ❖ Find out if there is a Kids Against Animal Cruelty chapter close to you.

- ❖ How can you use social media to spread the word about animals in dire need of homes in your own community?

- ❖ Look at the Kids Against Animal Cruelty website and discover what their coat of arms stands for. www.kidsagainstanimalcruelty.org

- ❖ Can you create your own coat of arms that states your own positive traits by which you wish to live?

Fire Rescue

Super Teen Hero, Latrell

14 year old Latrell was lifting weights at his friend's house late one Friday night, a regular way to spend his weekends in Fairfield, California. When he smelled smoke inside the apartment, he traced it to next door. The smoke was billowing out of the door. He grabbed the fire extinguisher and sprayed it around the door. He knew a disabled man and his dog were inside. He remembered learning that there was more oxygen under the smoke.

He went down on his hands and knees. Latrell crawled in and woke up his friend's neighbor, who was drowsy with smoke inhalation and dragged him outside onto the apartment building's walkway, away from the flames. Then, the neighbor said, "My dog, my dog". Latrell knew he had to go in again. Crawling once more, he managed to find the dog and carry him under his arm.

Latrell was outside taking deep gulps of air when the firemen arrived. The fire was hosed out and that is when the news cameras showed up. They interviewed a calm Latrell in front of the yellow "Do Not Pass" tape, behind him was the burned out interior hallway. The newsclip was sent to me by someone who knows that Animal Hero Kids is always looking for brave, courageous, and compassionate acts.

43

Chapter 5

Snatched from the Jaws of Death: Hugo

Mother, Brenda Weber, and her 14 year old daughter, Mattie, were at the Hernandez County Animal Services in central Florida looking for a cat to adopt. A white nose with streaky caramel coloring poked through a dog kennel gate opening to say hello as they walked by the dog area. Mother and daughter read his name was Hugo. Then mother and daughter went to look at the cats. A short while later they walked by only to see an empty cage and Hugo's bedding, water, and food dish were gone. They realized that in such a short time the chance of adoption was very slim. They both ran to the front, "Tears started flowing and we started running," said Wendy Weber, "We ran in the front office and screamed, 'Where is Hugo, we want Hugo!'"

Center, the Weber sisters each by a dog.

An employee ran across the shelter, shouting, "Don't euthanize Hugo!" When she reached the room where he was, Hugo had already been given anesthesia and was unconscious. Minutes away from death, Hugo was saved.

Hallie, Mattie's sister and Mattie both created Misfit Animal Rescue when they realized the large number of dogs and cats who need homes.

Animal Hero Kids were thrilled to recognize the Weber sisters for their dedication at a mass adoption event. We were amazed to learn that since the Weber's formed Misfit Animal Rescue, they have saved thousands from certain death at shelters. All of these animals are now enjoying their forever homes. When the teens received their Animal Hero Kids Award, they also received a $750 donation towards providing low cost spaying and neutering operations in their county. Misfit Animal Rescue now offers low cost spay and neuter of cats and dogs to prevent the birth of unwanted kittens and puppies.

Please go to misfitanimalrescue.com to learn more about the Weber sisters' work.

47

Tatiana, the Life Saving Dog

Animal Hero Kids recognizes lifesaving feats by four legged heroes too. It was in the middle of the night that Tatiana, a black mixed breed dog woke up and knew something was definitely not right. She was new in the home, yet, she still realized that the daughter of the family, Cristina, was struggling to breathe and needed help, quickly. Tatiana ran to the sleeping parents' room and woke them up. Tatiana's frantic movements alerted Cristina's parents that something was very wrong. They called the paramedics immediately when they saw Cristina in the throes of a severe asthma attack. The paramedics said that Tatiana had saved Cristina's life by a matter of minutes by getting medical help to her just in time.

Animal Hero Kids had to give Tatiana a Christmas present of a big basket of veggie dog biscuits and an Animal Hero Award at the Greater Miami Humane Society.

Animal heroes can be non-human animals too.

Tatiana is eyeing the dog biscuits Animal Hero Kids' Co-Pres Dominic is holding, as Cristina and Susan look on. In the background, Animal Hero Kids Role Model Stefan Kleinshuster, from Chapter 9 mountain rescue, looks on.

Did You Know?

🐾 A pitbull dog in Indiana stopped a burglar from leaving a couple's house with their baby.

🐾 Dogs are rescued from shelters in California to be trained as search and rescue dogs if they show they do not give up when looking for a toy.

🐾 Two stray dogs lay beside a woman who was stranded outside in the snowy wilderness with a hurt leg and kept her warm until help came.

Activity Ideas!

🐾 Can you research and find other instances where dogs saved the lives of humans?

🐾 Can you think of ways humans can return the favor and save the lives of dogs?

🐾 Does your local hospital or retirement home have therapy dogs?

Chapter 6

The Returning Hero Award

Animal Hero Kids recognizes four-legged feline heroes too. The Returning Hero Award recipient may have triumphed over tragedy or selflessly helped someone else. I was amazed by the actions of this one brave and adventurous cat.

Here is Holly's incredible story told by Holly's human guardian, Jacob Richter.

"Holly arrived in our life as a feral kitten healing from wounds she received from living inside an air conditioner unit from the fan; she jumped up on my mother's lap as she sat on her porch chair. This was Christmas Eve of 2010, how could I refuse her need? We took her in and after Christmas took her to our veterinarian. She got all the needs for a kitten. When the time was right, she was spayed and a chip inserted. We bonded with love and respect."

Jacob Richter in the center, with Holly's Returning Hero Award. To his left are the Weber sisters. Laura is AHK's kind, silver voiced singer on far right.

It was in November of 2012. The Richter family was vacationing in Daytona when Holly ran out of their recreation vehicle. They searched the local animal shelters, posted flyers, and delayed their trip home as long as possible. Fireworks exploding the day after Holly was lost may have scared her even further away. After exhaustive searching, still no Holly. Heartbroken, the Richters had to return home.

They received a report of a cat with the tortoiseshell cat's distinctive markings eating in Daytona Beach at a community cat colony about two weeks later.

One day about a month and a half later, Barb Mazzola and her daughter saw a thin cat in their yard. It took days to slowly convince the tortoiseshell with distinctive markings to trust them enough to eat. A vet's microchip check led to the ringing of Jacob and Bonnie's phone on New Year's Eve day. Holly had lost 75% of her body weight; the pads on her feet were scraped from walking on cement. The first thing Holly did when she returned home was to jump up on to Jacob Richter's lap. Jacob and his wife Bonnie say that "Holly's journey home was a miracle of love." Holly had walked from Daytona Beach racetrack to a home one mile north of the Richter's, just under 200 miles. Yet she made it home, a real life incredible journey.

Jacob told me about the scrapbook he was making for Holly when we spoke. He was thrilled to discover that Animal Hero Kids will recognize Holly with the "Returning Hero Award" which came with a gift certificate of $250. Jacob used the $250 gift card towards funding treatment for a shelter dog with an untreated broken leg. Star, a female German shepherd mix, nicknamed Love Bug, has found her forever home. She runs and plays with no trouble and is now Holly's gentle canine brother.

Jacob Richter was presented with the Returning Hero Award at an adoption fair to hang above Holly's cat bed. Jacob was glad to meet other Animal Hero Award recipients and Animal Hero Kids volunteers.

Activity Ideas!

❤ Discover other true stories of cats or dogs finding their way home.

❤ Think of ways to educate others about the importance of micro chipping companion animals.

❤ Can you write or create your own incredible journey story?

LONG BEACH, Calif. ABC7 Cool Kid for Thursday, July 17, is William Yuth, who is tackling pet overpopulation.

Yuth sees how the problem spirals out of control, when people treat their animals as a way to make money instead of as family pets.

"What happens is when you start to breed them, you have eight puppies. You try to sell them, no one's going to buy them, and they just end up in the shelter and eventually they get euthanized," Yuth said.

To prevent that fate for innocent animals, Yuth is volunteering with the group "Fix Long Beach." He takes the message directly to the people in his community.

"We went knocking on doors, asking them if they have any pets. We offer free spay and neuter services. Then we tell them where to go, then we direct them to this clinic."

🐾 Cats can see up to 6 times better than humans in the dark and only need 1/6 the amount of light a human does.

🐾 Cats' back legs power them upwards to jump onto surfaces way higher than humans can jump to.

🐾 Cats can jump 6 times higher than the length of their tail.

🐾 Cats and dogs greet each other with head bumps and tail sniffs.

🐾 A gradual introduction of a new four legged member of the family is best.

🐾 Monitored community cat colonies are a name for when people feed, vaccinate and spay or neuter outside cats. They used to be called feral cats. Their name was changed to encourage people not to interfere with their care by banning their feeding or trapping them. TNR stands for Trap, Neuter and Return; this is a humane way to care for cats that are used to being fed outside.

The day Gillian took Holly home.

Chapter 7

Holly and Gillian, a Foster Story

When I first met high school student, Gillian, she was wearing a t-shirt that said "Chickens are not nuggets." Gillian Robertson's Dad works at the Humane Society of St. Lucie County. She had become used to hearing the stories her Dad told her of the animals who end up at the shelter.

Gillian saw this one dog story on the evening news about a grey female pitbull, mixed breed dog that was tied to the back of a truck and dragged. It was horrific and sad. Gillian saw Holly had lots of injuries to her legs and paws when she visited Holly at the Humane Society. Gillian volunteered to take on the delicate, time-consuming job of nursing Holly back to health.

Holly's first day out

Holly was fostered by Gillian at her home so she could keep on changing her bandages. Slowly, Holly began to trust humans again. Until, finally, four months later I met Holly on her first day out at an adoptathon at a park. See the photo from that day at left.

Holly eventually found her forever home and is happy and safe at last.

Gillian also volunteers at a horse rescue and advocates boycotting rodeos. When I was contacted by the Nickelodeon Channel for Animal Hero Kids to speak out against animals used in entertainment, Gillian was chosen to speak about rodeos. She outlined the use of the bucking strap tied tight around the horse's lower extremities to force the horse to buck in pain. She also explained the cruelty of calf roping which jerks the infant cows' legs or neck backwards at sometimes up to speeds of up to 40 miles per hour, all the while she groomed Jimmy, a rescued horse who was overworked and injected with steroids at the racetrack.

Gillian was one of the people recognized with an Animal Hero Kids Award at an annual awards event. Sixty people were treated to veggie burgers, sweet potato fries and moon pies from MacN Truck, a vegan food truck.

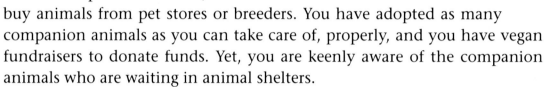

Putting Your Time Where Your Heart is

Let's say you want to help companion animals who are in shelters waiting to be adopted. You have told everyone how important it is to spay and neuter companion animals, how vital it is not to buy animals from pet stores or breeders. You have adopted as many companion animals as you can take care of, properly, and you have vegan fundraisers to donate funds. Yet, you are keenly aware of the companion animals who are waiting in animal shelters.

All animal shelters rely on volunteer help. Fraily Rodriguez from the Pet Alliance of Greater Orlando wrote to me about one of his teen volunteers. Rachel Gosselin truly puts her time where her heart is. Here's what he wrote me about Rachel's dedication.

Rachel started coming to our summer camps when she was in 7th grade. She became so passionate about the work we were doing that her mom begged us to have her volunteer for us. Rachel began volunteering as a freshman at our shelter and has logged over 500 hours for our animals. She comes in to walk the dogs and give them some individual attention. She has worked with our Behavior Department as an assistant through behavior classes and in enrichment projects. She has served as junior camp counselor and mentor for the last four years. Rachel has become so passionate about the cause of caring for homeless companion animals that she wants to continue to give back. She was accepted to Harvard University and will be enrolling as a freshman this fall. Her goal is to be a veterinarian and actively provide quality care.

"Animals don't care how old you are, so why should age determine what someone can and can't do to help them? If you are motivated enough, you can accomplish anything, no matter your age," said Rachel.

Bailey is 3 years old, she's a mutt, and we adopted her from the Pet Alliance of Greater Orlando when she was about 8 weeks old. I bring her to summer camps to help kids learn how to be responsible and respectful towards animals so, I guess you can say she's a volunteer making a difference too!

petallianceorlando.org

Classroom in Action

Beverly Wolfe's Diamondview Elementary School Companion Animal Club learned about the high numbers of domestic rabbits and baby chicks who are abandoned after being bought at pet stores for Easter after I gave a humane education presentation at their school. The students decided to act, and do something about the situation for rabbits. They created flyers, posters, and distributed them not just at their school but all over their community. They created their own bunny public service message for their school announcements in the weeks leading up to the Easter holiday asking people not to buy chicks or bunnies for Easter. The students definitely got the message out about not going to pet stores and buying animals. Many students, teachers, and parents changed their hearts and minds.

... both humans and animals live together in the same community. It is important to care and respect animals as if they were our friends because they also live in this world. Animals live with us, have emotions and are a part of this community.

CEDRIC, 14

PHOTO VOICE
Culebra 2013

Chapter 8

Double Twin Power for Animals

Lovey and I surprised twin sisters Alexandria and Sidney Cohen during their school assembly. We were doing a presentation about how everyone can be heroes to animals when we presented the sisters with an Animal Hero Award.

One of the many things the vegetarian sisters do to help animals is to speak at city commission meetings. Here's a summary of their speech asking the city to ban the sale of puppy mill dogs.

The twins addressed the commissioners speaking at the podium. They told them of how many homeless, stray dogs they have seen at animal control and the Humane Society. They said that if pet stores would stop selling dogs it would make the shelters' work much easier. "Every day, healthy adoptable animals are killed in the shelters only because there is no space." The commissioners listened attentively. This was only the first meeting set to discuss this issue. When the commissioners have their second meeting and make their decision, we will add it to the animalherokids.org News section. So stay tuned for further developments. No matter what, the Cohen sisters will never give up. They will speak, clearly, for those with no voice with double determination.

Did You Know?

🐾 Puppy mills are mass breeding operations where dogs are overcrowded in cages and bred for puppies for commercial sale.

🐾 In some instances the mother dogs don't ever feel grass under their feet and always stay in a cage.

Chapter 9

A Tall Tale of a Mountain Rescue

One day, a mountain climber in Colorado, named John Steed, was climbing a rocky, snowy mountain when he saw in the distance a dark shape near a rocky overhang. The shape moved. John realized the lonely far off shape was a dog, a German shepherd mix, who was trapped 6,000 feet up. He could not get close enough to help the dog. Stefan Kleinshuster, another mountain climber, read a post on a climbing website calling for help to try and find this stranded dog.

A group of veritable strangers came together with the same purpose. After a lot of strenuous rock climbing, finally, a pair of ears and a head appeared above an outcropping of rock. The closer the rescue group got to the dog, the more concerned they became. The dog's feet were wounded and she was obviously weak from being stranded out in the cold.

Amazingly, the kind and determined group were able to get up to her. The dog was weak, yet glad to see them and thankfully drank water. Now, the question was how to get the dog who weighed about 85 pounds down a ragged, 6,000 feet steep mountain face. The dog was placed in a backpack with her head sticking out. It was a slow, difficult journey, with lots of rest breaks. Finally the dog, named Lucky by the crew, was saved! After a stint in the local pound, Lucky is now living happily ever after with John Steed.

John's Animal Hero Tip is:

"We all have a duty to help those who can't help themselves and this often includes animals. If you see an animal in distress, please notify an adult whom you can trust like a parent, a teacher or even a policeman. You can make a difference and maybe even become an animal hero!"

Stefan Kleinshuster, one of the brave rescuers, was flown to Florida by Animal Hero Kids. We addressed two schools and gave Stefan an Animal Hero Kids Role Model Award for him and the other rescuers. This brave group also appeared on the Ellen Show to tell their wonderful story.

Stefan Kleinshuster in back row 2nd from the left, John Steed sitting to the right of Stefan, with their entire mountain rescue crew

Activity Ideas!

🐾 Have students create a pyramid of needs for companion animals. They can put a large sheet of paper on the wall or on the board and write in and draw as many details as they can think of: adequate food and fresh water, shelter, access to veterinary care, a family, companionship, walks, flea medication, collars, etc. This activity may be particularly successful in younger grades though in older grades, you may wish to team up with the art teacher and have older students produce a long mural to post in the hallway of your school.

Chapter 10

Special Friends with Special Needs

Animal hero kid, 11 year-old JP, has written about his own story...

The Day We Rescued Bella!
by JP Dyben

As the car drove down the freeway, I tried to picture what type of dog I should get. "Perhaps a spotted one or a really hairy one," I said to my mom.

She laughed and said "A big dog equals big poops," then laughed some more.

"Ew, gross!" I proclaimed.

When we got to the dog shelter, I saw tons of dogs and cats all over; some going in and some going out. I walked into the shelter and found myself in a waiting room. "Wow," I thought, "It's so bright in here." After a few minutes of checking in we were off to see the dogs. As I went to the back with my mom and Bill, my step dad, cool air blew in my face. I looked around. The room was not what I thought it would be. Gray walls and unhappy dogs gave sad looks as they banged on their gray chain cages. I was terrified. "Was this really what a dog rescue center looks like?" I wondered to myself. They let us outside where I played with dog after dog after dog.

Yet I felt no loving connection with any of them.

We walked into the waiting room again where the exit was. Feeling defeated, I asked "Aren't there any more dogs?" I suddenly heard a small scratch. I looked up to see a small dog behind an office door. Bill said, "There's one left, but it's blind." "Let me see it! She's blind? No one else will want her." As the small Yorkshire terrier was brought out by a woman, she said, "Now be careful, she is completely blind." I didn't care though. And let me say, it was love at first sniff (since she couldn't see). "This is the one!" I told my parents. "Are you sure?" Mom asked me. "Yes, Mom!" I told her "I love this dog!" Mom smiled and said "I'm sure she loves you too!" That is the story of how I met my lovely little dog Bella.

When Logan received his award at the Earth Day festival, he spoke to 1,000s of attendees.

"When you buy pets from breeders instead of from shelters, you leave shelter pets to die. There are too many animals and the shelters are out of room. We should find homes and families for the animals that don't have one instead of leaving them to die and giving money to people to breed more. A lot of those animals end up in the shelters too."

You will meet Ronnie V Cow pictured with Logan, Kitty T Cat, and Susan Hargreaves in Section 2, so read on.

"If you see someone hurting an animal, tell someone you trust! Don't be quiet! You're their only voice!"

Logan sleeping with rescued blind bulldog, Edison.

73

Two animal hero tips from Jorja Fox:

1. Be patient with people. People can be frustrating.
    Try not to take them personally and don't give up
    on people's ability to do good.

2. Take time to take breaks from your 'cause/issue' and play.
    Play regenerates you, helps you burn off frustration, and
    many good ideas come to your brain when your brain
    seems to be taking a break.

*Jorja Fox,
star of* CSI
*with the
apple of
her eye,
Bexar.*

"Your dog is your partner. Treat him like a partner. If you're not respecting your animals, you're not respecting yourself. Do not leave your animal out in the cold."
-Russell Simmons

Would you like your own animal hero story to be included in the next volume of Animal Hero Kids — Voices for the Voiceless? Please e-mail us your story at: education@ animalherokids.org.

Activity Ideas!

- Brainstorm all the different types of handicaps and special needs that affect human and non-human animals.

- How can companion animals with handicaps or special needs be accommodated to help them live rich, happy, fulfilling lives (for example, specialized carts for amputee dogs)?

- Would you like to start your own Animal Hero Kids crew in your community and get your friends together to help animals? Go to animalherokids.org to find out how.

Winners of the "Be Kind to All Animals" Poster Contest

Rose and rescued rooster at Farm Sanctuary

Chapter 11

... A little help from my friends

Animal Hero Kids loves trailblazing role models like Sir Paul McCartney.

Sir Paul McCartney is the recipient of the "Animal Hero Kids Kind Lifetime Award." He inspires people of all ages to be compassionate towards all species of animals. The former Beatle has been a vegetarian for over 30 years. Thanks to Paul's Meat Free Monday Campaign in the United Kingdom more schools are choosing to go veg. Here's his message to you...

"ANIMAL HERO KIDS ROCK!

It doesn't matter how young or old you are, the good news is you can help animals in need."

- Sir Paul McCartney

Animal Hero Kids is proud to name

_____

As the recipient of the Paul McCartney Young Veg Advocate award for assisting farmed animals in crisis, human health, and the planet.

Your work helping the most abused group of animals on the planet is vital.

It takes courage and compassion to be a voice for the voiceless!

Animal Hero Kids

Voices for the Voiceless

Fostering empathy and kindness in children and youth by encouraging and recognizing compassionate and courageous acts that help all species of animals; and offering complimentary, interactive, humane education.programs highlighting stories of the rescue and aid of animals in need.

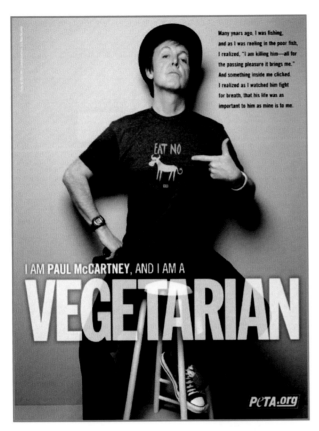

Many years ago, I was fishing, and as I was reeling in the poor fish, I realized, "I am killing him—all for the passing pleasure it brings me." And something inside me clicked. I realized as I watched him fight for breath, that his life was as important to him as mine is to me.

I AM **PAUL McCARTNEY**, AND I AM A

VEGETARIAN

PeTA.org

"If slaughterhouses had glass walls, we'd all be vegetarian." ~ Paul and Linda McCartney

A message from Animal Hero Kids role model - Sir Paul McCartney:

Hello to Animal Hero Kids, parents, and teachers. If you are reading this book chances are you want to help animals and the planet. Thank you. It was a nice surprise that Animal Hero Kids, the volunteer humane education group chose me for the "Animal Hero Kids Kind Lifetime Award."

One day many years ago we were on a sheep farm watching through the window the lambs playing around, just born, they were running saying to each other "Let's run back" and racing from one end of the field to the other. Then we realized what we were eating, a leg of lamb, we were eating an animal just like the lambs who were playing outside our window.

That's when I became vegetarian. Then I read the United Nations Report on global warming called Livestock's Long Shadow. I learned an animal based diet is not good for the planet, this was not a report from a vegetarian group, and this study was from the United Nations. I wrote letters to people I thought had influence, heads of state, people who can help make change.

The nominee search is on for an individual or group under the age of 19 for the Sir Paul McCartney Young Veg Advocate Award.

I heard about Meat Free Mondays that was already growing in other parts of the world. I thought it was a great campaign to get involved with. I found that people were looking for ways to help. Kids know that something has to be done about climate change knowing that it's their world that the grownups are messing up. Younger people particularly say we really love this idea — it gives a way to help save our future, a way to save our planet.

We are keen to get this idea into schools; many schools have adopted this idea. The Los Angeles Unified School District Superintendent, Dr. John Deasy, was just given the "Animal Hero Kids School Hero to All Award". The second largest school district in the United States serves over 65,000 meals every Monday and not one of them has any meat.

This will cut down on the billions of animals that are slaughtered for our consumption, every day, every month, and every year. Compassion was the thing that turned me into a vegetarian. Maybe we have a responsibility to do something for our children, for our fellow beings on this planet and for the future, for the generations to come. If you think this is a good idea then, please, help spread the word.

 meatfreemondays.com

* Animal Hero Kids is on the search for the winner of the Sir Paul McCartney Young Veg Advocate Award for an individual or a group under the age of 19 who has succeeded in proclaiming a message, far and wide, about the multiple positive aspects of a vegetarian diet.

* You can nominate or find out more details at animalherokids.org.

* It takes about 300 gallons of water per day to produce food for someone who is totally vegetarian. It takes more than 4,000 gallons of water per day to feed a meat-eater. Vegetarians save an acre of trees every year. More than 260 million acres of U.S. forest have been cleared to grow crops to feed animals who are raised for meat, and another acre of trees disappears every five seconds.

* Factory farming is a term created to describe the practice of treating animals like they are in a factory which contains thousands of cows, pigs, and chickens.

Activity Ideas!

🐾 Can you create a 60 second to 2 minute YouTube commercial about Animal Hero Kids' search for award nominees? Please, include details of how people can fill out the nomination form on the website and what categories exist. Classrooms can split into groups of four; each group can take one of the reasons outlined earlier that people are choosing to go vegetarian. Research facts about the effects animal based agriculture has on the environment, human health, the humane treatment of animals, and world hunger. Write and create your own commercial and each group "plays" the commercial for the class. Please, post your commercial on YouTube with the title Sir Paul McCartney Animal Hero Kids Veg Award.

🐾 Look up the definition of vegan and create a daily menu for a vegan.

Five Easy Steps
to Meat Free Mondays

Hundreds of schools have adopted Meat Free Mondays around the world.

1. Students propose the idea to a student council, or the Guidance Counselor or Head Office or make it a project of a student club.

2. Adults can discuss Meat Free Monday at parents' evenings and staff meetings.

3. Consider the menus with the catering department or, if your school uses external/council caterers, see if they are able to offer a MFM menu. Give sample recipes when needed.

4. Once you're good to go and have a start date simply sign up on meatfreemondays.com

5. Your school will be able to display the MFM logo on your website, receive regular MFM updates and be added to the growing list of participating schools.

 Go to meatfreemondays.com for more details.

Animal Hero Kids' free kindness presentations conclude with a vegan hero sandwich making activity.

Ronnie V Cow loves it when people eat vegan food. He helps with Animal Hero Kids' free, humane education programs. I bet you can guess what the letter V stands for in Ronnie V Cow's name – V is for Vegan.

Photo by Carla Wilson

❧ There are four main reasons people choose to go veg. Going veg helps: the animals, the earth, human health, and world hunger.

❧ A vegetarian saves an acre of trees a year.

❧ Animals on factory farms are the most abused group of animals in the world.

❧ Going veg reduces the chances of a heart attack, stroke, diabetes, certain types of cancer, etc.

❧ It takes 14 pounds of grain to produce one pound of meat. If you used that grain for pastas, bread, and cereals instead, you could feed 13 more people.

Activity Ideas!

❧ Physicians Committee for Responsible Medicine (PCRM) is a group of 6,000 physicians who keep updated on the effects diet, pesticides, and antibiotics have on human health. Research the world health graph to find out what number is the United States on the world life longevity list. pcrm.org

Chapter 12

"We Can All Be Heroes, We Can All Be Brave"

Eight year old Aaliyanah is Animal Hero Kids resident dancer. She dances to her own song called, "We Can All Be Heroes, We Can All Be Brave" at Animal Adoption Fairs around the east coast of Florida.

Aaliyanah is a great vegan spokesperson for animals. In the Animal Hero Veg Kids video on the website, she energetically tells everyone about how healthy she is. She loves to eat her fruits and veggies, her favorites being strawberries and bananas.

Aaliyanah was presented with an Animal Hero Kids Award for her advocacy work for animals. She speaks at municipal government hearings and meetings urging the adoption of humane laws. Her sincere words have the power to change minds.

We Can All Be Heroes, We Can All Be Brave

The animals are hurting
The time is now

I say animals
You say matter

We Can All Be Heroes, We Can All Be Brave

The animals are hurting
The time is now

I say animals
You say matter

Whistle Blower Saves Piglets

Imagine if you were in a group of friends who thought it was fun to be cruel. Would you be strong enough or brave enough to act in the victim's defense? There is one teen whistleblower who was. Eight baby pigs were rescued thanks to the teen's quick action. The piglets were being used for paintball target practice.

One piglet had already lost an eye when she was saved before any more harm was done. Thanks to this whistleblower telling a trusted adult, the piglets are safe now in a sanctuary today called Rooterville: a place where a pig can sniff, play, and be a pig! Visit **rooterville.org**.

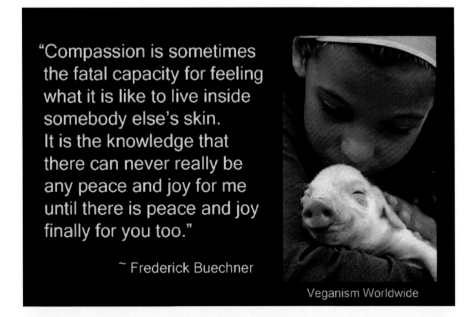

"Compassion is sometimes the fatal capacity for feeling what it is like to live inside somebody else's skin. It is the knowledge that there can never really be any peace and joy for me until there is peace and joy finally for you too."

~ Frederick Buechner

Veganism Worldwide

*MUSE students caring for the
environment through action*

Chapter 13

Kind Schools Rule!

California is the state to accomplish many "firsts." The Los Angeles Unified School District (LAUSD) was the first district to adopt "Meatless Mondays" to reduce animal suffering, the negative environmental impacts of factory farming and to improve healthy choices for students. LAUSD Superintendent Dr. John Deasy was awarded the 2013 "School Hero to All" Award.

Sir Paul McCartney relayed a special message to Dr. Deasy. "Bravo to Los Angeles School Superintendent Dr. John Deasy, the School Hero to All Award recipient, for making the decision to go meat-free each Monday in every school cafeteria in the second largest school district in the United States. Dr. Deasy, it is thanks to you that other school districts are jumping on board to help animals, the environment, and human health every Monday."

MUSE School is the recipient of the Animal Hero Kids School Hero to All Award for being the first school in the U.S. to serve completely plant-based food in their cafeteria.

Suzy Amis-Cameron, wife of *Avatar* and *Titanic* filmmaker, James Cameron, and her sister Rebecca Amis are founders of the MUSE School in Calabasas, California. MUSE School grows their own vegetables and, in 2015, will be the first school in the United States to offer all plant-based food. Students interviewed by ABC news in their school's vegetable garden expressed their agreement with eating a healthier school lunch.

The Animal Hero Kids School Hero to All Award recognizes individuals who go above and beyond benefitting animals, both two-legged and four legged and the Earth. Suzy Amis-Cameron, James Cameron, and Rebecca Amis are trailblazers. The MUSE School founders are achieving a groundbreaking first with the mindful decision to consider farm animals' wellbeing, human health and the environment by transitioning to a plant-based diet. Animal Hero Kids is proud to give the 2014 School Hero to All Award to MUSE School, Suzy Amis-Cameron, James Cameron, and Rebecca Amis.

*It takes courage and compassion
to be a voice for the voiceless.*

Kind2All Award Winners, Hialeah High School's Humane Initiative Club successfully petitioned students to vote for a Meatlesss Mondays program in their school cafeteria.

California Middle School Students Kind to All Animals

"Cause for Paws" is the school helping animals club at Fedde International Studies Middle School. Club members petitioned tirelessly to have Meatless Mondays adopted by their cafeteria. The students gained 325 signatures saying "yes to Meatless Mondays" out of a school population of approximately 390. Building on their recent victory for farmed animals in the ABC School District, the students are asking the whole school district to adopt a veg menu.

The students also help companion animals by directly rescuing cats and dogs found in their neighborhood in trash cans and the back of stores. Animal Hero Kids presented them with a Kind 2 All Award at the Los Angeles Animal Hero Kids Awards in 2013. The students were thrilled to hear Dr. Deasy, the Superintendent of their neighboring school district, speak about why they adopted a vegetarian Monday policy. Cat Hugar, the Fedde International's school club sponsor said " I am so proud of my students for making the connection between being kind to animals and going veg. They acted on their conscience and made a real difference."

Baby Chick, Revived to Thrive

Megan Ely is a hard-working high school student who still manages to volunteer many hours a week at the Pelican Harbor Seabird Sanctuary in Miami. On one of her weekends there she was called up to the front intake desk and asked to help a little orphaned chick who was in danger of dying. When babies do not have the comfort of a mother, or the warmth and comfort from another being, they can easily die.

There was no mother hen to adopt this baby as one of her own. Megan became the little chick's main caretaker, taking the infant with her, whenever she could. Megan became a vegetarian after realizing that each individual animal has a personality, like her canine and feline companions at home. When the little chicken grew, Megan realized he was a rooster with beautiful red, coppery feathers. The chick that grew was called Kevin. In the Florida noonday sun during Megan's lunch break at Pelican Harbor one of the staff snapped a photo of them both napping.

Megan regularly attends demonstrations for marine mammal freedom. She promotes not eating animals, and volunteers tirelessly at animal rescues. I surprised Megan at her high school with an Animal Hero Award for her work helping all species of animals. Megan continues to be a consistently compassionate champion of animals in need. She is currently in college pursuing her dream to rescue marine mammals.

- Chickens were originally native birds in Africa; they roosted in tree branches at night.

- Mother hens and chicks talk to each other while the chicks are still in their shells.

- Today, hundreds of millions of chickens don't have the room to stretch their wings. Chicks have the first half of their beak cut off right after they hatch, and are kept in the dark in a large building.

- Hatcheries are places where hens lay eggs. When their babies hatch from their eggs they are on moving conveyor belts and if they are male they are gassed or suffocated since the egg industry does not want birds who don't lay eggs.

Activity Ideas!

- Classrooms can split into four groups and research the number of products that contain eggs, and then find replacements for them. Find out from Physicians Committee for Responsible Medicine (PCRM at pcrm.org) how much cholesterol is in eggs and how cholesterol affects human health.

Go to unitedpoultyconcerns.org and choose one story or issue to relay to the class.

Chapter 14

Help a Horse? Of Course!

Alexandra Gritta was 15 years old when she stood, transfixed, in the middle of a herd of rescued horses at the Duchess Sanctuary in Oregon.

She heard the story of the mares in the herd and their babies being rescued from the cruel pregnant mare urine (PMU) industry, and then the mares are sold and used in the drug industry. Orphaned mustangs, and horses rescued from auctions and feedlots also make up the sanctuary's population of about 200 horses who are free to run on the 1,120 acre sanctuary run by the Fund for Animals and the Humane Society of the United States.

Alexandra decided to help; she formed her own non-profit book publishing company, Charity Book Series, and began to write for the horses. To date, $25,000 have been donated to caring for rescued horses. She has also made her own documentary informing others about the PMU industry.

Alexandra says "I decided to speak out because I believe most women do not realize that the hormone replacement therapy drug Premarin® actually stands for PREgnant MARe urINe, and that it is a billion dollar industry built on horse abuse and slaughter."

To find out how you can help all horses,
go to the equineadvocates.org website.

Visit fundforanimals.org/duchess-sanctuary for many beautiful touching stories of horses saved.

To find out more about Alexandra's books, please go to alexandragritta.com.

To find out more about Panhandle Equine Rescue, please go to http://www.panhandleequinerescue.org/.

Kylie, who is 8 years old and Avery, who is 4, are two sisters with heart. They had seen Panhandle Equine Rescue on the news. At their birthday parties, they asked for money to donate for the horses. They raised just over $200. They were so excited to drive out to the rescue and hand delivered the donation and the two bags of apples we brought for a treat. Kylie received a big kiss from Comanche, one of the rescued equine residents.

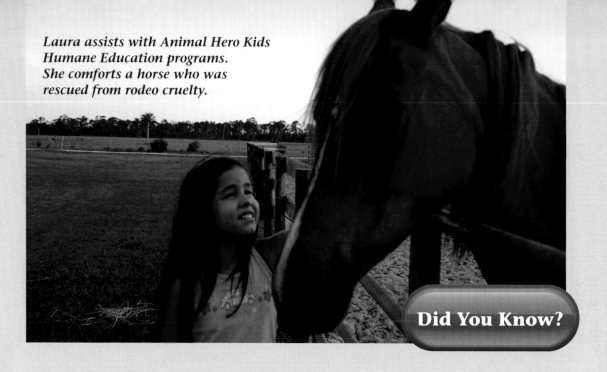

Laura assists with Animal Hero Kids Humane Education programs. She comforts a horse who was rescued from rodeo cruelty.

Did You Know?

- A horse is a member of the "equus" family. This word originates from the Greek dialect, and means 'quickness'. Equus caballus, is a term given to modern-day horses.

- Horses, calves, and bulls used in rodeos are treated inhumanely. A strap is tied very tightly around the lower abdomen of a horse. This is called a bucking strap. The horse tries to get that painful tight strap off and bucks. Calves are roped and pulled up to 40 miles an hour, sometimes ropes jerk their bodies or necks backward and they are wrestled to the ground.

- Foals have milk teeth, just like human babies. At around age 3, these teeth start getting replaced by permanent teeth.

- Horses can sleep lying down as well as standing up. They sleep only 3-4 hours per day.

Activity Ideas!

❧ Organize a "bring a blanket or apple or carrot" party for a horse rescue near you. Invite friends or ask your class or school to have a day where you bring in a gift for the horses.

❧ Write a letter to President Obama and thank him for not funding meat inspectors for horse slaughter.

❧ Ask your representative to support the SAFE Act, which will keep American horses safe from being shipped to Mexico and Canada for slaughter. Please, send a polite letter to your U.S. Representative and to two U.S. Senators.

❧ Find out who your representative is by going online and entering your zip code on this site. http://www.house.gov/representatives/find/

❧ Can you design your own ad or poster showing how to be kind to horses? Post your ad on community bulletin boards, or make a video about how others can help horses. Please only post on social media sites with the approval of a trusted adult.

Chapter 15

"I love these teens!"
-Miss Piggy

One day, I heard on the television news an announcer say...

"Five high school students took on the school board today pleading to save the lives of their pigs, one school board member, Frank Cobo, citing his history of having a pet pig when he was a boy voted for the pigs, the other members, however, voted against the pigs. They will be sold for slaughter at the Dade County Fair". I saw tears rolling down the faces of five teen girls who had just failed with their heartfelt plea at the Dade County School Board. As they spoke with the reporter I learned how they had cared for the pigs since they were baby piglets.

The Coral Reef High School students had raised the domestic animals from babies and then were expected to end their class project by ending the lives of their hoofed friends. The fate of these animals was not going to be a happy one, as you can imagine. The teens did not give up and began raising their own funds to buy the pigs back.

During the Dade County fair bidding, with over three hundred dollars in hand, Leonor Armas, Natasha Patter, Tanya Reddy, Ana Mendieta and Lori Hussein began their bids. A coach at the school was determined to buy the pigs to kill and roast them. He raised the bidding number past the point of the students' financial limit. It looked like all of their efforts would come to no good when a true animal friend who had seen the students on the news pleading for the lives of their four-legged friends raised his hand. Steve Rosen began to bid, each time the coach bid, Steve would raise his bid until finally the pigs were saved.

Thanks to the courageous, caring actions and generosity of five Coral Reef High School students, the outcome for four lucky animals was a much happier one. Four animals were saved from certain slaughter that night thanks to the caring actions of Steve Rosen and the students.

Jasmine Speaks Out for Pigs

Jasmine, Animal Hero Kids Canada President, looking into pig slaughter transport truck in Toronto.

Jasmine, a young activist gathers with other activists to give water or watermelon to pigs on the way to the slaughterhouse in downtown Toronto with the local animal protection group Toronto Pig Save. This group documents the conditions of the pigs with cameras.

This picture was taken on a busy street corner in Toronto. Many trucks pass each day carrying pigs to a local slaughterhouse. I take part in these vigils so I can help educate people about what happens to the animals used for food, and to ask one very important question. "Why do we love one but eat the other?"

These animals feel pain and fear. All you have to do is look into their eyes when they are in the trucks or waiting to be killed at a slaughterhouse. They know what is going on.

If you think kids can't make a difference, try telling that to Jordan Star who, at 15, got devocalization (removing animals' ability to make sounds) banned in Massachusetts, or Monica Plumb who, at age 10, began petmask.com providing oxygen masks for animals, and has saved many lives. There are heroes all around us. You can be one yourself. Never think your voice doesn't matter, because many our age are making a big difference all around the world. –Jasmine

Jasmine and her mom with some very lucky pigs at the Wishing Well (Farm Animal) Sanctuary in Bradford, Ontario. http://www.wishingwellsanctuary.org/

Young Jasmine works to save all species of animals, including wildlife and factory farmed-animals. She creates YouTube videos to educate people about how they can be heroes to animals.

Pigalina the piglet with friend Levi the pit bull at PIGS Sanctuary

Orphaned Piglet and Rescue Dog Develop Unlikely Friendship

At the PIGS Animal Sanctuary in West Virginia, an unusual friendship has blossomed. Pigalina the piglet and Levi the dog may not be the same size - or species! - but they love hanging out together.

After Pigalina was rejected by her litter, she began living with the other animals at the sanctuary — one of whom is Levi, the pit bull terrier rescue. Pigalina has become fascinated by the big dog, and even though Levi likes to play it cool, it's pretty obvious that these two friends complement one another nicely.

Here's hoping that Pigalina continues to make many new friends at the sanctuary!

Kevin Storm Makes Waves on the Radio

When Kevin was 11 he started hosting his own radio show. He called and asked the WNJC 1360 AM radio station manager in New Jersey if he could have his own show. Now he is 12 years old, he said he saw footage from people, who went undercover to film how farmed animals are treated. When he saw the cruelty, he became vegan. "It's like selective favoritism towards animals.

We see a cat and say "oh, cute" Yet, farm animals are cruelly treated and no one sees it. It's behind closed doors and then the animals end up in little packages." Kevin speaks to his classmates about what is happening to factory farmed animals and how inhumanely they are treated. He showed one friend "Meet your Meat" which made him go vegan, too.

Kevin's mission is to spread the word about going vegan, and says it is the most powerful step you can take to help everyone, animals, the planet, our own health, and world hunger. Since, you can feed more people with a vegan diet than a meat-based diet. On one acre, you can produce 20,000 pounds of potatoes or 150 pounds of cow meat.

"I can't imagine who came up with the thought. The animal was probably doing no harm, sitting there minding his/her own business. Oh, the animal is weaker than me, I can do whatever I want, we're more important than they are and now we are force breeding, and think we have the right to use them any way we want," said Kevin, on one show. Kevin normally travels to the radio station to do his radio show.

Occasionally, he will also broadcast live from places he's visiting. Kevin may have been nervous when he first began hosting his own show; however, he's determined to speak clearly and directly, for the animals who have no voice and no choice.

Did You Know?

- 🐾 Many great speakers, heads of state, celebrities, and even animal advocates get nervous before going on the microphone.

- 🐾 Elephants, bulls, giraffes, rhinoceroses, gorillas, moose are all proof you can grow big and strong on a vegan diet.

- 🐾 Drinking cow's milk can contribute to ear infections, runny noses, and digestive problems. Soy, almond, rice, and coconut milks are now widely available in U.S. and Canadian grocery stores.

- 🐾 The best kind of calcium for the human body is in green leafy veggies, orange juice and nuts.

Young people have more power than is almost imaginable because everybody who is selling something hopes young people will buy, or push their parents to buy, whatever foods, clothes, games and more that they are selling. And that power can be used to change the animals' world, their fate, just by saying "I won't go to Seaworld or the animal circus; I would like the bean taco, not the meat one; and I wear vegan sweaters and shoes.

-Ingrid Newkirk

Activity Ideas!

❖ Create your own radio show. Decide on a name, a subject, and what type of animal or animal hero you wish to interview. For example, if you wish to interview someone like Emily, the cow, who is in the next story, what type of questions would you ask her? What would her answers be? If you are in a middle school or high school class, assemble into four different groups, and create your own radio show that can educate about how others can help farm animals. After you have practiced, roleplay the radio show for your class. The rest of the class can vote on which radio show can be played on the school announcements or which will be recorded.

❖ Organize a debate on the topic of the treatment of farm animals. Have two groups research their arguments for and against the current treatment of animals on intensive (factory) farms and on smaller traditional family farms. Ask permission to hold the debate in front of the entire student body.

Chapter 16

Emily, the Cow who Saved Herself

Imagine being in a life threatening situation where the only thing you can do to escape is to jump over a five foot gate, without knowing what was on the other side. Emily, the two-year-old female cow, was at the end of being used by the dairy industry. Most mother cows have 6 babies, each calf is taken away at one day old so humans can drink her milk.

If the calves are male they are put in crates which are so small that they are unable to turn around. After enduring this confinement for 16 to 18 weeks, they are killed for the veal meat trade. Emily kept going to the back of the slaughterhouse transport truck, when the other cows were being prodded off the truck through the iron gate on a large loading dock. She heard and smelled

fear; she was headed where all the other mother cows go after their milk is sold.

Emily was one very scared and motivated cow. She jumped over the iron fence and into the neighboring forests in Massachusetts. Emily ran for her life. She made friends with other hooved creatures in the forest and neighboring people put food out for the deer and for Emily. For five weeks, Emily hung out with her new `wild` friends.

Though the company who owned Emily was looking for her, none of the neighbors said they saw her. Emily was a cow hiding out, undercover. She was on the news, a cow celebrity with the story of her daring escape from death. A vegetarian family heard of her plight on the television news. It was winter and Emily was getting thin, and so they began looking for Emily. The Randa family ran the Peace Abbey, a place where people gathered. A safe home was waiting for Emily where she would be treated with care and respect.

Finally, on Christmas Eve, Emily was convinced to go into the Randa's trailer, it was as if she knew that the Randa's little girl and her Mom and Dad were her saviors. Emily lived her life at the Peace Abbey and I met her when I was there for an Earthsave conference. Big beautiful eyes with long eyelashes, a black cow with an island of white on her forehead, Emily attracted visitors from far and wide, who had heard of her story. Emily lived a serene existence with other cow and two-legged human companions.

A statue was created in honor of Emily's bravery and courage when she died. Emily reached many people with her story, and in this book, Emily, the legend of the cow who saved herself, continues.

Chapter 17

Whitney and Chicklett: A Liberation Story

Whitney tells her story in her own words...

At the beginning of the high school semester we were told we were going to be buying baby chicks, raising them for 5-7 weeks, and then slaughtering them. When we were told this, it was too late to transfer classes. Assuming we didn't have enough funding for the project I wasn't too concerned. Then all of a sudden we had boxes filled with baby chickens, and we were told to pick our own chicken. I believe this was wrong, we were never asked to fill out a permission slip, and we were told to raise and kill our own chickens.

When the word raise is brought to mind, what do you think of? When I hear the word "raise," I think of taking care of something or someone because they cannot do it on their own. This involves baby animals; they cannot raise themselves, especially not in a cage. So, we chose our chickens, gave our chickens names, and found ways to remember which chicken belonged to which person.

While everyone else was covering their chickens in permanent marker, I was looking at my chicken's color. My chicken had an orange head instead of yellow, which is what all the other chickens had in my group. So I could distinctly tell the difference, but Mr. Hamilton made me color mine anyway. I didn't want to color my chicken with a permanent marker because it felt wrong. If coloring the chicken made me feel bad, how do you imagine killing it would make me feel? So, instead of coloring my chicken, I put a purple dot on his foot; it still felt wrong, but it was a lot better than covering his feathers in purple marker.

So, I had chosen my chicken, given him a name (Chicklett), and now it was time to raise my chicken. I helped the group feed and water the chickens every day, sweeping the messes off the floor, and weighed my chicken every week to make sure he was gaining weight properly.

I took pictures of my chicken as he grew, and still, without marker, I could tell him from the rest. My chicken had become a loved one; no matter how stupid that sounds, he had. I am an animal lover, I have a dog and he's like my son. I go to the zoo and it makes me cry because the animals look so depressed and lonely. So yes, I have, in fact, become attached to Chicklett, and could not participate in his death.

If you cannot understand my feelings, let me put it in perspective for you. If you have a pet at home that you love dearly, or if you have ever had a pet that you loved, then look at it like this; someone throws your pet in a cage with 4 or 5 others, and says that in 5 weeks you are to cut off its head, pull off its fur, clean out all the guts, bag and freeze the meat, and take it home for your family to enjoy – what would you do? Would you not do everything in your power to keep a loved one safe? Are pets not loved ones? I acted on the grounds of love and empathy for another living being. I raised my chicken. I decided I would not kill him, but skipping the killing wasn't enough, how could I save him?

In school dissection there is almost always a choice of doing an online version. But we were told that we must do some part of the slaughtering. Yes, to some he is just a chicken, but to me he's a living being and has just as much right to live as we do. There is a choice in dissection, why not in the slaughtering of an animal you raised?

There were several moments throughout the project when I told my teacher that I wasn't going to do this, I didn't want to participate and that I wanted to keep Chicklett. I was never excused from the "broiler project." Tears became a normal ending to most of my days during these weeks. The time grew nearer and my pain grew stronger. I began telling my friends and family that I was just going to take Chicklett and put him into my purse, but I didn't really think that I would.

The more I spoke out, the more some students would begin to make fun of me. My job was [supposed] to [be] pluck[ing] the feathers from my chicken and other chickens' dead bodies. I began picturing Chicklett's lifeless body… The weekend before the scheduled Monday slaughter; I talked and cried to my mother. I decided that I didn't have to slit Chicklett's throat just because I was being told to. I would never have forgiven myself had I decided to be a follower and kill the animal I raised, fed, cared for, named, and that I loved. Chicklett trusted me.

I love the sweet sounds he makes when you hold and cuddle him. I knew that weekend that I had no other choice but to rescue Chicklett and get him to a safe place.

After Whitney met Chicklett, she became vegetarian. Whitney says "I found out that the bottom dollar and speed of output outweighs human compassion for the animals on factory farms today. I believe the solution lies in exposure and education; one by one the message to stop promoting, buying, and eating abused animals will be heard.

The day came that Whitney had been dreading for so long. Shortly after Whitney arrived in class, she quickly placed Chicklett in her large purse and exited towards the doors, and met her Mom who was waiting for her outside in the car.

 Whitney also wrote a poem from Chicklett's point of view. Here's an excerpt, for the full poem, please, go to animalherokids.org.

> *Just a Chicken*
> *So you think I'm just one chicken,*
> *One less meal on your plate.*
> *But my purpose now is greater,*
> *And that's a much better fate.*
> *My final message is a gift to the world,*
> *Please open up your eyes.*
> *See finger lickin' for what it really is,*
> *One giant pack of lies.*

Whitney says, "My chicken has become a loved one." And: "I will not apologize for what I have done. I will not regret it, and I would definitely do it again if I had to." In a letter sent to the school, Karen Davis, an educator and chicken sanctuary director, wrote... "A society that recognizes the greatness of Martin Luther King, Rosa Parks, and other fearless moral leaders of the past must cherish Whitney Hillman. It is easy to venerate pioneers of the past. Whitney Hillman is in the present, and she is definitely the hope of the future."

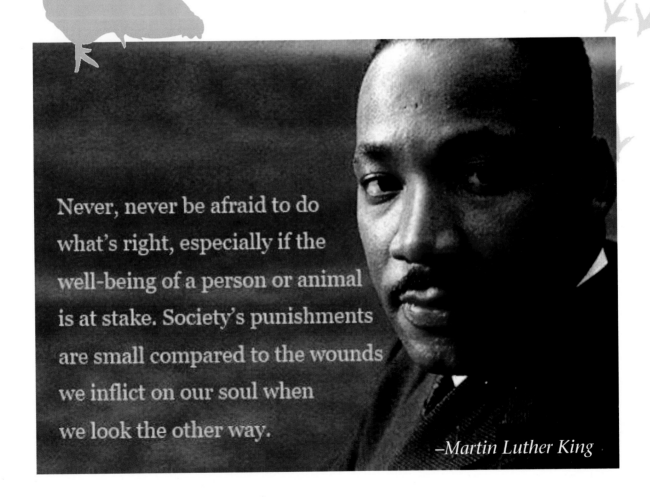

Never, never be afraid to do what's right, especially if the well-being of a person or animal is at stake. Society's punishments are small compared to the wounds we inflict on our soul when we look the other way.

–Martin Luther King

A representative of Veggie Grill, and Chef Scot Jones of Crossroads Kitchen congratulate Clara.

Chapter 18

Saving Lots of Cows and Pigs, and Chickens... Oh My!

Clara Polito was 5 years old when she found out where real hamburgers and steaks come from... or who they came from. When her mother told Clara this truth she became vegetarian. When she was 11 years old she found out the cruel truth behind the cows' milk industry. Here's what Clara said in her own words about baby male cows being taken from their mothers a few hours after they are born, and put in veal crates where they cannot turn around, and are fed an iron deficient formula then killed at 16 weeks of age.

"I think it's really gross to consume breast milk from cows that was meant for their babies, who get separated from their mothers within a couple of hours of being born. It's easy to be vegan today. Get your parents involved, even just one parent. Research what you're doing and explain it thoroughly to your parents. If they don't get it, tell them the horrid facts you've learned about dairy and factory farming. Explain to them that it's not going to cost more money, probably about the same, and find more affordable places to shop that provide plenty of vegan options. Becoming vegan was probably the best decision of my life!" When Clara was 12 years of age she created her own vegan baking company. She experimented in her own kitchen and found the perfect recipes for her own line. In Los Angeles, Animal Hero Kids gave Clara the Kind Entrepreneur Award for the creation of her caring company called Clara Cakes.

At the 2013 Los Angeles Animal Hero Kids Awards, the Veggie Grill restaurant chain gave Clara a gift card that included free food for one year. Clara's cupcakes are now being sold in local stores. Clara never let the fact that she was 12 years old stop her from making a difference, and encourages all who meet her to do the same. Clara is following her dream and helping animals one cupcake at a time!

The little piglet on wheels, which help him walk, is looking up at a sheep friend at Edgar's Mission, a farm animal rescue, in Australia.

A Surprise Sponsor Gift for Nestor

Heres a story about a group of young enterpreuners who raised funds to assist animals in need.

Kayla Worden, founder of Full Circle Farm Sanctuary in Asheville, North Carolina, told me about a recent day when she was feeling tired from caring for all of the farmed animals saved at her sanctuary. Here's what she told me...

I went to the post office and saw this envelope from someone in Chapel Hill, NC. When I opened it and found this lovely, hand-written card with beautiful images of farmed animals drawn on it, I was moved to tears upon reading the heartfelt words written by students.

I knew that the school Animal Rights Club's donation should go to sponsor one of our hoofed residents. I knew who right away. A little special needs goat.

Nestor was viewed as a liability and a profit loss by the goat farmers who were using him. They were planning to take his life because he was partially blind. After a kind person called and asked us to intervene on his behalf, we picked him up. Tragically, animals caught up in the food machine in this world continue to have their true worth overlooked as they are routinely abused and cruelly exploited. I was so glad to be able to save Nestor, this one little goat, who needed a quick rescue.

When I introduced Nestor to the other rescued animals, he immediately made friends with Nemo the llama. Nemo now comforts Nestor and they are close friends.

I realized a group of school students from more than halfway across the state, that had never met me or had even been to our sanctuary, cared. They took it upon themselves to make the world a more gentle, compassionate place for farmed animals. Well, that just touched me deep inside my heart. We are a small, all-volunteer operation. It means the world that these lovely students would make such ongoing efforts in this meaningful way. I am moved beyond words and ever so grateful to them. They are inspiring and give me hope for the future of our world. They are making a true difference and are a bright light in the darkness. My heart goes out to them and I send them my most sincere thanks for putting their compassion into ACTION in such a meaningful way.

Carly and Felicity with the Durham Animal Rights club tell why they decided to raise funds for farm animals...

"I can still remember sitting in my room sobbing after seeing how animals on factory farms were, and are, treated. I saw pigs in gestation crates so small they could barely move and male chicks being thrown into grinders. I couldn't stand to see these animals in the conditions they were in and I wanted to help in any way I could. I decided to start a club at my school. I truly believe that if more people knew how badly the animals are being treated in factory farms, many of them would also have similar beliefs and would want to make a difference. The Animal Rights Club has allowed other students with similar beliefs to get together, raise awareness of animal abuse and mistreatment, and raise money to help animals in factory farming. Next year, we're planning to have a fundraiser where we will sell delicious cruelty-free food. I was a little scared to start the Animal Rights Club because I didn't want anyone to make fun of me for something I cared so much about. When I set up my stand at the club fair, however, more than forty people signed up." -Carly

"We made it our club's mission to raise money and donate it to facilities that take abused farm animals and give them a safe haven where they can recuperate and eventually thrive." -Felicity

Chapter 19

How Stella Got Her Groove Back

Rebecca was 12 years of age when the phone rang in their rural Grant, Florida home. A neighbor had just discovered a bruised, scratched, thin and extremely dehydrated female pig, collapsed in his yard. "She looked terrible, I knew I had to help in any way I could" said Rebecca.

She had a missing tail and a stapled number tag in her ear, so, they knew she had been used on a farm for breeding since her tail was cut off, standard practice on factory farms. Her scratches and cuts could have been from scraping on the road when she fell off a slaughterhouse transport truck. They call it road rash. But one thing was obvious, she needed water badly!

The day Rebecca first saw Stella

They dragged the water hose out as far as it would reach and began to make a giant puddle of muddy water in the yard. Their piggy guest was weak but she used what little strength she had left to drag herself towards the water and her salvation.

As Robyn, the mother of Rebecca, puts it, "She (Stella) allowed Rebecca to pet her while she was drinking some water and after getting sprayed with the hose she laid down and took a mud bath for a while. That is when Rebecca named her Stella."

Stella was moved down the street to live with Rebecca's family. They had plenty of space so that Stella could graze and simply enjoy the wide open space. Her weeks there were completely opposite of her previous living conditions at the factory farm.

When she was kept as a breeding pig she didn't even have enough space to turn around let alone lay down. With Rebecca's family she had more space than she would ever need. At the factory farm it seemed she was never fed enough to stay at a healthy weight, since she was so thin. Now she got to feast on grain, bread, carrots, hay, and her favorite food, grapevine leaves.

Stella received the kindness and love that, before meeting her rescuers, she had never experienced before. However, they could not keep her, so a kind neighbor named Sue knew of a sanctuary for pigs named Rooterville near Gainesville, Florida. Stella was safe for the rest of her life in her forever home.

Stella's life was changed, for the better, when she was rescued but also when Rebecca gave her love. Something as simple as the communication between children and animals is often seen as being inspirational, even miraculous. Rebecca didn't just give Stella her name or pet her when she was hurt; she showed Stella that you can still hope. Rebecca taught Stella that some people will hurt and break you but others will help and heal you.

Most of all, Stella got to experience the unconditional love of a little girl. Which some people say is the most amazing thing anyone, human or animal, can ever have!

Source for photo: http://www.rooterville.org/index.php/animal-stories/stellas-story

Eryn, who wrote this story, is Animal Hero Kids' 14 year old reporter.

© 2014 Jessica Chastain

I don't normally get into this, but I'm a vegan. And I try not to, well, I don't want to torture anything. I guess it's about trying to live a life where I'm not contributing to the cruelty in the world... While I am on this planet, I want everyone I meet to know that I am grateful they are here. –Jessica Chastain

133

- James Cromwell the actor became vegetarian after starring in the movie *Babe* as Farmer Hoggit, and has since rescued a real-life Babe from slaughter by buying the pig at a stockyard when he heard of a class of kids who did not realize the pig they raised was going to be auctioned off to be killed.

- The average American will eat 21 cows, 1,400 chickens, 12 pigs and 14 sheep in their lifetime.

- A pig's sense of smell is so keen that in France people who pick truffle mushrooms for a living have a pet pig to help them sniff out the mushrooms.

- When pigs roll in the mud they are using natural sunscreen to protect their sun-sensitive skin.

- There has been more than one occasion when pigs have saved the lives of their human companions by waking them up because they smelled smoke.

- Jessica Chastain, Hayden Panetierre, Kristen Bell, Natalie Portman, Kate Winslett, Alicia Silverstone, Christina Applegate, Ellen DeGeneres, Pamela Anderson, Samuel L. Jackson, Alec Baldwin, Brad Pitt, Woody Harrelson, Russell Brand, Tobey McGuire, Ed Begley, Jr., Joaquin Phoenix, Christian Bale, and many more famous celebrities are all vegetarian.

- Carrie Underwood, Shania Twain, P!nk, Gwen Stefani, Sir Paul McCartney, Bryan Adams, Jack Johnson, and Jared Leto (along with his entire band: 30 Seconds To Mars) are among hundreds of famous vegetarian and vegan musicians.

- Go to famousveggie.com and make a list of actors, musicians, and athletes and see which list is longest.

- Have a *Babe* or *Babe 2* or *Chicken Run* watching party where you enjoy veggie dogs, veggie burgers, with Soy Delicious cones or Tofutti Cuties, frozen creamy treats available in most major grocery stores in Canada and the U.S.

- A lot of mainstream movies exist and popularize the idea of the kind treatment of farm animals, freeing farm animals, and how humans can play a positive role.

Those who dismiss love for our fellow creatures as mere sentimentality overlook a good and important part of our humanity. But it takes nothing away from a human to be kind to an animal. And it is actually within us to grant them a happy life and a long one.
–Joaquin Phoenix

135

Amazing Grace

Molli was 13 years old when she saw firsthand what happens to dairy cows. Molli's mom, works at Gentle Barn, a sanctuary for some very fortunate farm animals who were rescued from the factory farming industry. Here's her story…

"When I first saw Grace, I saw hurt and fear, and anger. I saw someone who had been betrayed and treated with the most tremendous unkindness to the point where not one kind word or action could be taken to heart or understood. Whenever I tell Grace's story to anyone, their mouths drop open in astonishment at how much pain she has been through, both physically and emotionally. It literally is hard for people to hear about how much pain and suffering could be inflicted onto one being, but then they get to see that she seems to feel none of it now. Grace seems happy, and everyone can tell."

Grace spent 12 years being impregnated and having her babies taken away each year. Grace had 10 babies taken away from her after they were born, so, her milk could be sold for humans to drink. Then at the age of 12 she was bred to a very large bull who crippled her. Grace spent months trying to get up but to no avail. She was about to be sent to slaughter when The Gentle Barn intervened and brought her home instead. Gentle Barn staff and volunteers spent months treating her with massage therapy and chiropractic care until she could walk. Healing her body was relatively easy compared to what it would take to heal her heart. Grace had been disrespected by humans for so many years she had lost all hope. At first we ensured she had a lot of personal space and then slowly we began talking to her, singing to her, petting her and feeding her treats. Eventually she began trusting us and became less angry, but there was still pain in her eyes.

Grace needed someone special to fall in love with and I really wanted to help. I became Grace's docent on Sundays when the barn is open to the public. I stand in front of Grace explaining to visitors that Grace is not ready to be petted. I help guests feed Grace carrots and tell them her story which shows how brave and beautiful Grace is. Gradually, Grace has softened and found happiness at The Gentle Barn. She knows she is always protected and respected. Grace trusts me now and has let love in. Come visit The Gentle Barn any Sunday from 10-2 and you will find Molli and Grace together, teaching people kindness to animals, each other and the planet!

gentlebarn.org

Did You Know?

- Milk sold in stores is not allowed to come from a cow who is feeding her baby, which is why the cows have their babies taken away when they are a day old. If the calf is male, they are put in veal crates where they cannot turn around and are fed an iron deficient formula and then are taken out and killed at 16 to 18 weeks old.

- Bovine Growth Hormone is often injected into female cows to make their udders larger to produce more milk. This causes Mastitis which is an infection that often ends up in the milk.

- Many dairy farms are also veal calf farms.

- Research why there is a drop in the amount of cow's milk being consumed by people in the United States.

Chapter 20

Animal Hero Kids Fave Vegan Goodies: Bonus Vegan Recipes

The Boys in the Band - Kool2BKind

The Kool2BKind boy band is made up of three vegan animal activist brothers who love music. They like to listen to Pink, Green Day, and Nate Ruess. They play music and love to sing rock, pop, and punk songs. Ronan (age 9), Tristan (twin brother, age 9) and little bro Derrian (age 7) work up quite an appetite after a busy day of learning, singing, and playing.

Here are their favorite, healthy vegan meals without any ingredients that harm animals. They also love to order new vegan foods on those special occasions when they go out to veg restaurants.

Tristan's fave Indian-inspired burrito wrap

Ingredients
chickpea potato paratha
three spoons steamed basmati rice
seasoned cooked lentils (dark lentils with chili powder/curry/Braggs)
vegan margarine or vegetable oil and salt, pepper to taste

Preparation
- heat paratha in oven
- steam rice in salted water, add margarine, salt and pepper to taste
- heat lentils in pan with veg oil or melted vegan margarine, add salt, pepper, chili powder, curry powder, Braggs
- lay heated paratha flat on large plate, scoop three spoons of rice into a line down middle of paratha, pour 2 or 3 spoons of lentils over rice in line down the middle of paratha

Don't overfill!

Roll the paratha to make a nice burrito or wrap shape.
Full meal deal: eat with some steamed green beans and some raw veggies/hummus or salad for a complete meal.

Why would I eat animals? I love vegan food!

Ronan's Tofu Shells and Curry

Ingredients
bag of small pasta shells
bag of frozen organic peas
large package extra firm tofu
olive oil
salt, pepper, curry powder or paste

Preparation
- cook pasta shells in salted water till al dente (don't overcook) drain and set aside
- rinse tofu and cut in cubes, sauté in olive oil in large frying pan with salt, pepper, other spices as you wish
- add pasta back into pan with tofu cubes, add whole bag frozen organic peas
- add lots of curry powder or paste
- mix well on low heat and let cook for 5-10 minutes so peas get hot, add water or a little unsweetened soy milk to thin the sauce
- sprinkle with good-tasting nutritional yeast for extra zesty taste!

I don't eat anything that caused death or suffering.

Full meal deal: serve with vegan garlic bread, steamed broccoli, and tomato soup on the side.

Derrian's spaghetti dinner for a growing (vegan) boy

Ingredients
bag of organic (white or whole wheat) spaghetti
homemade vegan pasta sauce
Daiya mozzarella cheese, grated
organic vegan baked beans
multigrain bread
margarine/olive oil

Preparation
- cook spaghetti in salted water with a drop of olive oil, add margarine, salt, and pepper to taste
- heat 1 cup homemade vegan pasta sauce in sauce pan
- heat baked beans in small sauce pan
- toast two slices multigrain bread, spread thinly with margarine
- serve large spoonful of spaghetti onto large dinner plate, pour sauce over spaghetti, sprinkle with Daiya grated mozzarella cheese, put heated baked beans onto two slices of multigrain toast beside spaghetti on plate

In my family, we eat lots of good food and none of it hurt animals.

Full meal deal: serve with vegan bruschetta (optional), a crunchy salad or steamed broccoli, and coconut tapioca pudding topped with fresh fruit in season: mango, banana, berries for dessert.

Aaliyanah's Mac & Cheeze

Here's 9 year old Aaliyanah's message for you about vegan yummies. Aaliyanah was 6-years-old when she received her Animal Hero Kids Award for speaking to city commissioners to convince them to ban electro shock prods being used on elephants. Since then, she has helped animals, more and more, with her strong voice and her always kind choices for animal's wellbeing. Now at 9 years of age Aaliyanah is one of the Co-Presidents of Animal Hero Kids and volunteers on a regular basis to help inspire others to be kind to animals. You will also see Aaliyanah in Section 3 speaking up for dolphins.

"The reason I'm vegetarian is because animals get slaughtered. I feel they don't deserve it because they're just like us. There's no reason why we should kill them."

At school during lunch in the cafeteria the other kids ask me what I'm eating and I say, it's vegan ham, lettuce, tomato, and vegan mayonnaise. "What's vegan ham?" they ask, and I tell them you can get it in the grocery stores. They are interested, and there's no teasing.

I've got two favorite vegan meals, the first favorite is Macaroni and Cheeze, all vegan, from a restaurant called Darbster's, where you can even bring your dog in the restaurant.

My second favorite is Tofutti Chocolate covered vanilla soy ice cream cones, and in the bottom of the cone is a big piece of dark chocolate. It's delicious.

- A cup of pasta for each person is a good amount.
- Cook short, round pasta, in a pan as the directions on the box say.
- Then pour in unsweetened soy milk and sprinkle Daiya Cheddar Cheese shreds, and Follow Your Heart Monterey Jack Soy Cheese with a little margarine and nutritional yeast.
- Note: Nutritional yeast is good in soups, on popcorn, pastas, in salad dressings, and is full of B Vitamins, which is good for energy.
- If you want to make it even tastier you can add peas and bake with bread crumbs and nutritional yeast in the oven at 375° for 10 minutes. Make sure there's lots of yummy stuff covering the pasta, so, it doesn't get dry when you bake it.

Eryn, Animal Hero Kids Teen Reporter's Southern Chili

I first became a vegetarian because I would eat a burger or a chicken nugget and think, this is really weird and disgusting. And then I later started feeling really sad and sick whenever I thought about the billions of animals that suffer and are murdered for people to enjoy a burger. That's what is truly disgusting.

When I first became a vegetarian my family and friends would tease me about it asking me if I wanted a burger or something meat for a meal. But that was mostly because they didn't think I could last very long without eating meat. But I proved them wrong, when three years later, I'm still a vegetarian. Now when I tell people that I've been a vegetarian for so long it's as if they respect me for it.

You have to have a reason for not eating meat. You have to have a reason to resist the temptation of everyday meat eating. I do it for the animals, that's why my will to remain a vegetarian is so strong. When we lived in Kentucky I started making this recipe...

Eryn's Southern Chili

Ingredients

About a ¾ of a cup of
 crumbled veggie burgers
About 1 cup of green onions
About 1/2 cup of a bell pepper
14 1/2 ounce can of diced tomatoes
16 ounce can of kidney beans
15 ounce can of black beans
5 tbsp. of chili powder
4 tbsp. of olive oil
2 tbsp. of garlic powder
Dash of sea salt to taste *(Note: Can sprinkle nutritional yeast for more flavor.)*

Directions

1. Prep all of your ingredients by dicing the green onion, veggie burgers and bell pepper. Open all of the cans and measure out the chili powder.
2. Sauté the garlic, chili powder, veggie burgers. When browned, add bell pepper and green onion, save a little green onion for garnish.
3. Pour the red kidney beans, black beans and chili powder into the pot.
4. If you like your chili to be thicker, drain the tomatoes before adding them to your chili. If you prefer it soupy, then add the tomatoes as they come.
5. Now that all the ingredients are in the pot, mix everything together, stirring occasionally, for 1 hour.
6. Then turn it to low. Continue to stir occasionally until you are ready to eat.
7. Garnish with green onions, serve, and enjoy!

Arielle is an Animal Hero Teen who co-hosted the Animal Hero Kids Los Angeles Award ceremony in 2013.

"My generation is the world's future. The younger you are the greater impact you can have on future generations. Every person, no matter how young or old, has the power to encourage kindness and make a difference. If I can encourage even one person to stop eating animals, attending circuses or marine parks where animals suffer then I have made a difference."

Here's what Arielle drinks to recharge when she gets home from school.

Vegan Peanut Butter Chocolate Bliss Smoothie
2 frozen bananas
2 cups of chocolate almond milk
2 tablespoons of peanut butter
Blend and serve.

Tastes like peanut butter ice cream.
Arielle's mom is addicted to it too. It is soooo good!

No-Bake Mocha Chocolate Chip Cookies

Sky, wearing her favorite Animal Hero Kids t-shirt, visits CJ Acres Sanctuary. She visits her friend, Butterscotch, the goat. Butterscotch is sweet, and Sky has a sweet tooth. Here are her favorite mocha cookies!

Ingredients
2/3 cup quick oats
1/4 cup plus 3 tbsp oat flour
2 tbsp cocoa powder
1/4 tsp salt
1/4 tsp baking soda
1/4 cup sugar
1 1/2 tsp decaf instant coffee granules
1/4 cup chocolate chips
or mini chocolate chips
1/4 cup coconut oil
2 tbsp water
1/2 tsp pure vanilla extract

Directions
- In a mixing bowl, combine all dry ingredients and stir very well.
- In a cup, combine liquid ingredients, then pour wet into dry and stir until mixed fully.
- Transfer to a plastic bag and form into a ball.
- Now you can roll into smaller balls or put into the fridge until it is a little firmer.
- You could also bake these if you wish.

Jasmine's Vegan Key Lime Bites

Here is one of Toronto pig hero Jasmine's favorite recipes.

Ingredients
3 limes
2 cups cashews
3 tbsp. agave nectar
1/2 cup coconut milk + oil
1 sleeve graham crackers
1/4 cup melted vegan butter

Directions
- The only real pre-prep you have to do is soak cashews for 4 hours or overnight. The rest is done in the food processor and blender, starting with the crust.
- The crust is made up of 1 sleeve of graham crackers and 1/4 cup melted vegan butter.
- Put the two together in a food processor and then press into muffin liners (or make a large pie and use a glass pie dish). Then use a small glass or the back of a spoon to press down and get an even top. Finally, bake for 10 minutes till slightly brown.
- Once you blend your filling until creamy and smooth it's poured onto the crust and then the lime bites are put into the freezer. These only take a couple hours to make and the wrappers peel away easily for eating.

Vegan Birthday Party!

Princess Madeline Mary Francis and the Birthday Rainbow Layer Cake

A very special cake with multi-colored layers arrived at one lucky six year olds' house for her 6th birthday party. A sweet, fun time was enjoyed by all, except for a few tired adults at the end of the day.

Madeline says she's vegan because "animals are her friends, not food." She appeared in a video with her sign saying exactly how she feels.

A bright and yummy, vegan, layered cake for the true Warrior of the Rainbow!

- Prep time: 2 hr 0 min
- Total time: 4 hours
- Servings: 12 or more depending on slice sizes

This is easier than it looks if you use a vegan boxed cake mix, like Duncan Hines classic yellow cake mix.

Ingredients

2 boxes of cake mix
Rainbow colors of food coloring
8 ounces of Tofutti Better than Cream
Cheese plain flavor or Daiya
1 cup of vegan margarine
5 cups of powdered confectioner's
sugar (Now you know why the adults
were tired!)
1 tablespoon of vanilla

Directions

- In a bowl, mix the first cake according to directions replacing ingredients with vegan choices above.
- Separate batter into 3 bowls with approximately 1 cup per bowl, add food coloring to each bowl, purple, blue and green.
- Bake cakes in round pans after greasing them according to box directions, check cakes 10 minutes before they're done as the cakes bake faster with less batter.
- Take out and set to cool.
- Then do the whole thing all over again except with red, orange and yellow food coloring in the batter.

Some people may bake the cakes the day before and assemble the day after. Madeline's cake was green, blue, yellow and red colored layers. The choice is yours!

For the frosting, mix together softened vegan margarine, (prefer no palm oil in the margarine, you will read about chimpanzees and palm oil as an ingredient in Section 3: Wildlife Animal Hero Kids) and room temperature Tofuttu or vegan cream cheese. Add vanilla after combining and then slowly add sugar.

It's best to trim each cake to make the sides straight and even, after each layer of the cake is added after you spread the frosting with a spatula, put in fridge to set for 45 min to an hour, if you want to keep each layer from running into the next.

Then when the cake is frosted all around, leave in fridge for about an hour or more to set. Yes, that's a long time but the result is worth it! Now you know why we use a vegan instant cake mix... Whew!

Michel Estopinan, the Miami Hialeah High School teacher, sponsors the Humane School Initiative Club. Students work on issues related to justice and kindness for all beings. They have been discussing how to prevent Ad-Gag laws.

The students gathered support for Meatless Mondays in their school cafeteria, participated in the Walk for Farm Animals, and educate their school population about the impact their consumer choices have.

He plans to have students write letters to lawmakers asking them to not create laws prohibiting filming or photographing animals being harmed on factory farms, at stockyards, and in slaughterhouses.

☙ There is a Native North American Cree story about an old wise woman of the Cree nation, named "Eyes of Fire." She had a vision of the future. She predicted that one day, because of the white man's or Yo-ne-gis' greed, there would come a time, when the Earth was being polluted. There would come a time when the "keepers of the legend, stories, culture rituals, and myths, and all the Ancient Tribal Customs" would be needed to restore us to health, making the Earth green again. They would be mankind's key to survival... they were known as the "Warriors of the Rainbow."
Source: http://www.manataka.org/page235.html

☙ Ag-Gag laws is a term that means a person who witnesses animal abuse or documents it, is not allowed to tell others or show others the cruelty that is happening to the animals. There are brave undercover investigators who are working to show what is happening to farmed animals. Many incidents of video footage capturing abuse has been used to charge people with animal cruelty. That's why the meat, egg, and dairy industry representatives asked for Ag-Gag Laws. Compassionate people wrote their senators and newspaper editors and managed to defeat Ag-Gag laws in 18 States. Right now there are four states, Iowa, Utah, Missouri, and Idaho who have Ag-Gag laws where whistleblowers and investigators can be fined or jailed for showing what happens to animals behind closed doors.

Activity Ideas!

- Research which States are still considering Ag-Gag bills. Research instances where an undercover investigation has helped animals. People for the Ethical Treatment of Animals, and Mercy for Animals both have champion undercover investigation departments.

- Look up the definition of Freedom of Speech, and Factory Farming.

- Write a letter to the editor of your local newspaper to let them know that the freedom to stop animal abuse is being restricted.

- Discuss the "demand and supply" market and how an informed consumer choice can make positive changes.

- With a group of friends or in your class, brainstorm all the ways in which you can be Warriors of the Rainbow.

- Look out for how you can help animals every day of your life by thinking and researching the effect your consumer choices have.

- Change your diet to have less impact on the Earth.

"This may surprise you, because it surprised me when I found out, but the single biggest thing an individual can do to combat climate change is to stop eating animals."

~ Suzy Amis-Cameron and James Cameron

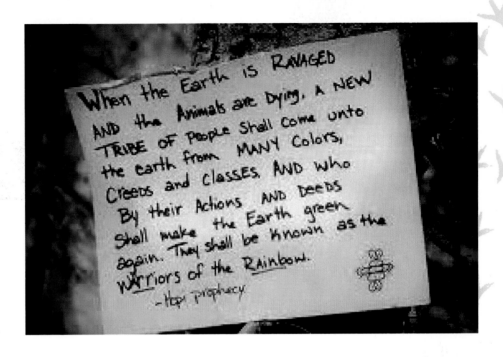

When the Earth is RAVAGED
AND the Animals are Dying, A NEW
TRIBE of People Shall come unto
the earth from MANY Colors,
Creeds and Classes. AND who
By their Actions AND DeeDS
Shall make the Earth green
again. They shall be known as the
Warriors of the RAInbow.
 -Hopi prophecy

*Genesis, a true warrior for all animals,
wearing her fave T-shirt.*

Winners of the "Be Kind to All Animals" Poster Contest

If a Warrior of the Rainbow were to film animals being harmed in a State that had an Ag-Gag law, what would could happen to him or her?

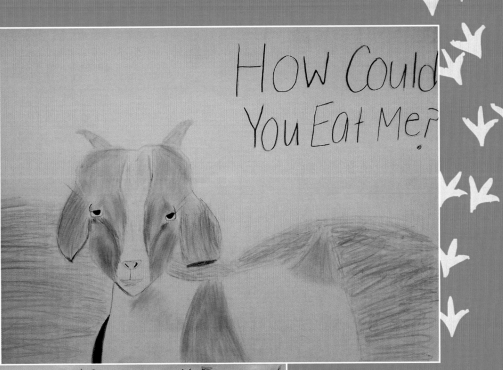

Chapter 21

Wild Animals Belong in the Wild

When you look up the definition of wildlife, the descriptions you find will include the phrase "wild animals living in their natural, undomesticated state." Yet we often see wildlife in circuses, zoos, and aquariums — a very unnatural environment. When I volunteer to present Animal Hero Kids humane education school presentations, I show two photos, one of a tiger in a cage and one of a tiger in the wild. A show of hands tells me which tiger the students would choose to be. I bet you can guess what their answer is.

When wildlife is taken from their natural environment and families, the mother is often killed protecting her babies. This is true for elephants, orcas, dolphins, chimpanzees and more. The good news is that there are Animal Hero Kids and teens speaking up for captive wildlife. When some young people discover the true story behind captive wildlife shows and theme parks, they act. One such example is the Film Arts class at Point Loma High School. Their creative YouTube video is getting the word out about the plight of captive marine mammals. They received an award from one of Animal Hero Kids adult role models, the Russell Simmons Creative Animal Hero Kids Award, in 2013, for their inspiring video.

We're Wild about Russell Simmons!

Philanthropist celebrity Russell Simmons was honored at the 2013 Animal Hero Kids Awards in Los Angeles for being kind. Russell Simmons is a vegan and entrepreneur who is known as the father of hip hop. Animal Hero Kids and Russell Simmons are both on the search for candidates who creatively inspire others to help animals in sad situations. Animal Hero Kids representatives, Russell Simmons and Oxygen reality TV star from the show "Running Russell Simmons" and animal activist, Simone Reyes, teamed up to honor creative kind kids and teens.

Point Loma High School students were one of two recipients of the Russell Simmons Creative Animal Hero Kids Award for speaking up for captive orcas in their video called "Dear SeaWorld." The students created the powerful video asking SeaWorld questions about holding orcas captive in tanks after they saw the documentary movie called *Blackfish*. You can see the video on the media page of animalherokids.org or Watch it here: https://www. youtube.com/watch?v=81Ihsvhx4-c.

Russell Simmon's winning creative category Dear SeaWorld video

More than 200 students attended the awards, some performed musical acts on stage with messages of kindness to all animals. Several young actors, including *The Twilight Saga*'s Booboo Stewart, *Trouble with the Curve*'s Lou Wegner (read about Lou in Chapter 4), and Disney's *Crash & Bernstein*'s Landry Bender and many more came to cheer on the Animal Hero Kids award recipients. Nominations are now open for the Russell Simmons Creative Animal Hero Kids Award category, so start creating!

 Please visit animalherokids.org.

Rose, Splashes Out for Orcas

Rose McCoy was 12 years old when she jumped in front of the SeaWorld float in the Macy's parade and the Rose Bowl parade. Rose feels the float's "orcas in the ocean" theme was ignoring the real facts about orcas in captivity. Here's Rose's story in her own words…

I know baby orcas are taken away from their loving moms, leaving them thrashing and wailing with grief. Wild orcas never permanently leave their moms and pods. It's awful for SeaWorld to separate mothers and children, which it does all the time.

Orcas and dolphins in the wild have the whole ocean to swim in, and they have dozens of friends and family members who love them. They are super-smart animals who work together as a team, talk to each other using special dialects, and swim for many, many miles every day, enjoying the currents and the sights of the sea. At marine mammal "abusement" parks all of this is taken away. Their world is shrunk from square miles to square feet. That's why I jumped in front of SeaWorld's Rose Parade float and the Macy's float to protest cruelty to orcas and dolphins.

Intelligent orcas with individual personalities are reduced to cartoon "Shamus." How many audience members realize that every single orca performer, male or female, in SeaWorld's parks is called "Shamu"!

Swimming in circles in SeaWorld's fishbowls makes orcas and dolphins crazed, frustrated, and angry. Who wouldn't feel the same way if they were kidnapped, imprisoned in a tiny tank, and forced to perform silly tricks on command?

There is nothing that aquariums who keep orcas captive can do and no one it can hire who can erase the truth that those of us who saw *Blackfish* know. Customers are running away from supporting jailing marine mammals! Ticket sales are down, musicians are canceling shows, and schools are canceling field trips. SeaWorld can never make up for the lives it has destroyed. The only thing that it can do now is stop hurting more animals and release the orcas it has to coastal sanctuaries.

Recently, California state lawmaker Richard Bloom introduced a bill that would force SeaWorld to do the right thing by making it illegal for SeaWorld San Diego to hold orcas in captivity.

I wish I lived in California, because I would like to walk right up to Mr. Bloom and give him a big hug. It makes me sad that instead of working to free orcas—to have them live in the great oceans again, they are kept in small, barren tanks. We don't want to see orcas and dolphins turned into circus clowns. Animals are so much better than that. We should be, too.

Megan from Section 2, Ric O'Barry star of *The Cove*, and Dominic in 2011

Orca's Get Out of Jail Free Card

Dominic, 11 year old Animal Hero Kids Co-president, does presentations for his school projects about helping animals every chance he gets. He began organizing protests when he was 8 years old, "I keep organizing one protest each month to educate the public about Lolita, the Orca, who has been kept in a small tank for 44 years at the Miami Seaquarium. She was stolen from the sea by the orca hunters using a series of small explosions to disorient her family. I don't think it's right to keep Lolita in the Miami Seaquarium instead of the sea. Animals are just like us, they don't want to be imprisoned and kept away from their family."

I will keep working towards setting all captive marine mammals free. What do we have to do to get them a Get Out of Jail Free card?

Dominic's five steps to organizing your own protest:

- Choose a place that's going to be effective. You want to be close enough to reach your target audience. Check where public property is.
- Set the protest up on Facebook or Twitter and get friends and other people to spread the word about why you want to protest.
- Make signs for people to use and leaflets about what you are choosing to protest against. Make sure you have water with you.
- Write a news release that is short and has just the facts with a cell number and e-mail address for contact. Tell the press that the protest is 15 minutes to 30 minutes later than it starts. It gives time for people to show up and for the event to be in full swing.
- Get to the protest early and make sure you thank everyone for coming. Lead the group by chanting with a megaphone, handing out leaflets. Have a sign-in sheet so you can contact the people who came for the next protest.

One of Animal Hero Kids free, interactive presentations "Free in the Sea" a play where kids create their own story for their class to watch.

Did You Know?

- Orcas used to be called killer whales even though they are the largest member of the dolphin family.

- Orcas have been living free in the sea for millions of years.

- There has never been a case where orcas have harmed humans in their native habitat, yet, four people have died in orca tanks. (Source: "Death at SeaWorld", *St Martin's Press*, 2012)

- The direction to swim and the search for food for orcas and other dolphins is accomplished by something called echo location or sonar waves. Sounds are made that sound like a finger running down the end of a comb, a type of clicking sound. When each click bounces off an object it is sent back and received and felt through the orca's lower jaw. This tells the orca where an object is located.

- Dr. Paul Spong has been studying orca pods who swim off the coast of British Columbia, Canada, since 1970.

- Lolita was taken from her family in 1970 from the San Juan Islands; she's now 50 years old. Lolita's great grandmother lived to be 103 in her natural home. Three of Lolita's relatives who were with her when she was captured are still alive, including an orca who is 86 and thought to be her mother.

Lolita's mother, Ocean Sun, has the distinctive open patch behind her dorsal fin.
Photo by Dave Ellifrit, courtesy the Center for Whale Research

🐾 The Orca Network records the sounds of Lolita's remaining pod family members and others, in the San Juan Islands, Washington State. They have each orca identified; no two dorsal fins or markings are alike. After years of captivity an orca's dorsal fin begins to droop.

🐾 Aquariums paint black sunscreen on the orcas, in the wild the orcas would not be in such shallow water and be exposed to the sun constantly. The black cream disguises the effect of sun damage, and peeling skin.

Activity Ideas!

- Investigate the effects on orcas of the consistent echoing return of sonar sounds from the walls of cement tanks.

- Investigate the different ways in which orcas communicate with each other. If they live in a matriarchal society, how long do orca infants stay with their mothers? Report your findings to the class. Orcanetwork.org and orcalab.org are good places to start.

- Set up a debate role play in the form of a televised debate between the scientists who are for orca freedom, like Dr. Spong, or Dr. Naomi Rose and public relation representatives of the entertainment theme parks who display captive marine mammals for profit.

- For more information, please visit the following websites:

- sanjuanorcas.com

- orcanetwork.org

- orcalab.org

Dominic organized protests against orca captivity. Left to right, Greer, Aoife and Dominic asking for Lolita's freedom.

🐾 Can you write a polite letter to Palace Entertainment asking the new owners of the Miami Seaquarium to release Lolita back to her family? See animalherokids.org for the address.

🐾 Feel free to draw a picture of Lolita returned to the sea.

🐾 Younger children can make their own costumes and create their own "Free in the Sea" interactive play about the return of a captured baby orca or dolphin to their family.

🐾 Hold a *Blackfish* viewing party, with vegan goodies. Conclude it with a brainstorming session about the best way to inform the public about the miserable, unnatural life captive wildlife leads.

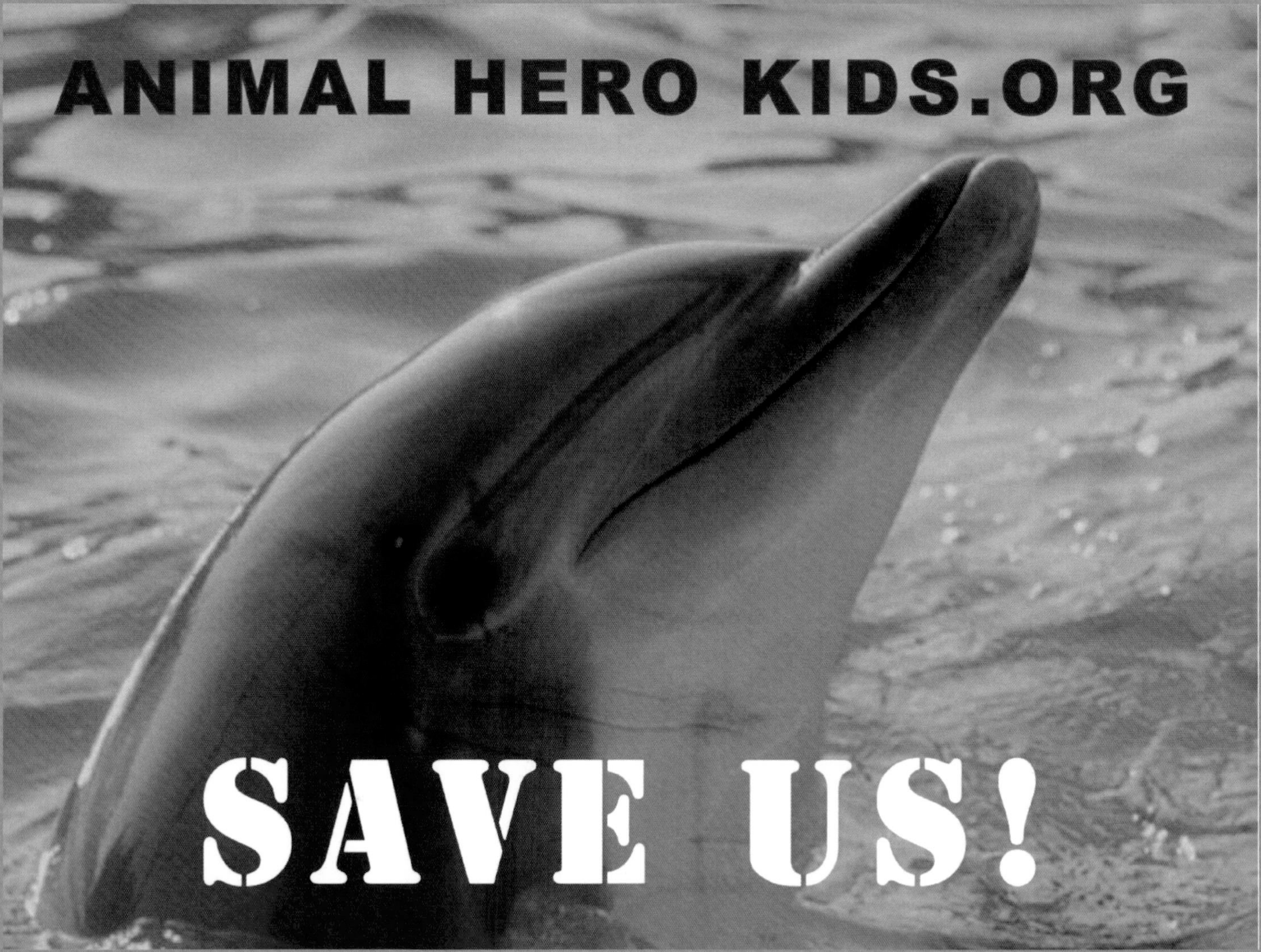
ANIMAL HERO KIDS.ORG
SAVE US!

Chapter 22

Dolphins in Crisis

Simone Reyes, another worthy Animal Hero Kids Role Model, was very pleased to join Russell Simmons to congratulate one of the young filmmakers of the Dear SeaWorld video on stage at the 2013 Animal Hero Kids Awards. Simone has loved animals ever since she could remember and is on a determined mission to encourage the kind treatment of all animals.

Simone has a story she really wants everyone to be aware of. Here it is…

"I have always marveled at those that document animal cruelty. HOW could they stand by and not stop animals being killed in front of

Simone as a young girl

them. I could never do that. No, not me. That was my belief and for many years that thought process kept me from going to the Cove in Japan. This is where Japanese fishermen drive dolphins into the bloody waters of the cove made famous by the academy award winning documentary, *The Cove*. They steal wild dolphins to become performing slaves while slaughtering the rest of the family for food. The meat of dolphins is dangerous to eat due to high mercury levels. This past November, I gathered up my courage and flew to Japan as a Sea Shepherd Cove Guardian. (The Sea Shepherd Conservation Society is the group behind Animal Planet's hit TV show *Whale Wars*.) The Cove Guardians film the Japanese dolphin slaughter in order to ensure the world is aware of what is happening to the dolphins.

My first trip to the Cove I remember this way: Climbing many stairs onto higher ground where we would have a bird's eye view of the cove. The Cove Guardians and I saw twelve banger boats (called banger boats because of the sound they use to drive the dolphins into the cove) terrorizing and chasing a pod of Risso dolphins. With every mile as the boats came closer we would hope that they would lose the pod. It has happened before. But the boats bang and disorientate the pod relentlessly pushing them toward the killing cove. This battle has at times gone on for several hours. Sometimes, the pod wins. Today, would not be that day. Today, the family of Risso dolphins put up a fight but many were terribly young—tiny babies even—and mothers/fathers were trying to stay close and protect their young.

Thirteen Risso family members eventually lost their battle and we saw them clinging together when netted into the killing cove. One got entangled in a net desperately trying to escape. Men in wet suits swam towards him and wrestled him out of the net and back into the cove with brutal force. The mothers and juveniles were almost attached they swam so close to one another, desperate to stay with each other. At one point the entire family was moving as one, trying to stay together in their last moments of life.

As we watched in horror documenting and live streaming video on the Internet, our eyes settled on two very young babies, their little fins so tiny

next to their protective and panicked mothers. Too small to be worth any money to the killers and, not wanting to have them counted as part of their quota, they cruelly drove them out to sea. It was then I knew my heart would never leave this cove. The babies were heartlessly ripped from their family and then thrown onto a skiff under tarps that hid Japan's shame. Our cameras caught a shaking terrified fin of a baby under a tarp, being stepped on and held still by the bodies of the fisherman killers. I couldn't hold back my tears that flowed from such a primal place in my soul, the only comfort coming from the occasional hand on my back of one of the Cove Guardians who had seen this before but would never get used to the killing before them.

Simone at the cove

Dominic and Ric O'Barry, former trainer of Flipper of the TV show by the same name and star of The Cove

I vowed in that moment to tell everyone who would listen about what I saw in Taiji that morning and to keep the plight of these dolphins and whales on the public's radar with every breath I would take from that day forward.

In the end, all of this violence against gentle dolphins can be blamed on "abusement" parks that offer dolphin/whale/orca/etc. shows and hotels and resorts that have swim with dolphin programs and those that buy tickets to shows. Taiji, Japan is ground zero for the captive dolphin trade. The meat, high in mercury, and often sold under other names is simply a by-product of this industry. The captive dolphins I saw, terrorized, depressed, scared, and begging for food broke my heart. They will haunt me forever.

I marched through the Valley of Death with the Cove Guardians of Sea Shepherd. I have seen the sickest part of humanity and will speak of it over and over until the citizens of the world begin to extend the "freedom for all" concept to every being. Nobody is free until everyone is free. This is something my boss/friend Russell Simmons tweets all the time. There cannot be peace in this world until there is peace for all. And so, we stand and we document and we rage against the machine. Loud. Relentless. Unified. Until every tank is empty."

Russell Simmons and Simone Reyes wrote a letter to President Obama and Ambassador Caroline Kennedy urging them to speak on behalf of the dolphins to the Japanese government. Oscar-winning performers Sean Penn, Cher, Susan Sarandon, Jennifer Hudson, Gwyneth Paltrow and Charlize Theron plus TV stars Ellen DeGeneres and William Shatner, and many others signed the letter, too.

One of the phrases in the letter was...

"Should human compassion not be afforded the same privilege as business interests? The world is looking to you, Ambassador Kennedy, and to our government to send a clear message to Japan that this atrocity must be banned now."

 Visit the Sea Shepherd Conservation Society's website at: sscs.org.

"These guys are so gentle it's like shooting a puppy dog. I don't see how there is any honor in that."

– Captain Paul Watson,
from *Whale Wars*

175

Give Them a Voice!

13 year-old Animal Hero Teen, Anna, from Yellowwood Learning Community and Animal Hero Kids' Co-Presidents, Dominic and Aaliyanah, teamed up to help the dolphins.

Here's Anna's story about her decision to help dolphins in crisis.

"During the spring of my 7th grade year, I watched the movie *The Cove* at school. I was shocked to learn that each year from September to May over 20,000 dolphins are slaughtered in Japan. Fishermen round them up by using sound barriers to disorient and herd the pods out of their normal migrations into hidden lagoons. Bottlenose dolphins, especially ones that look like Flipper, are pre-selected by trainers and sold off for around $200,000 to marine mammal parks around the world, where they will remain in captivity performing like circus animals.

The dolphins that are not sold as performers are inhumanely killed. The butchered dolphins are later sold as meat for food—meat that is actually contaminated with high levels of mercury, which is dangerous for human consumption.

My friends and I were so disturbed by the reality the dolphins in Japan are facing that we decided to go to the Japanese consulate and peacefully let them know that we wanted something better for these gentle animals. We chose to deliver Valentine cards on February 14 with Animal Hero Kids Co-Presidents Dominic and Aaliyanah. and Susan Hargreaves. It seemed like a simple, safe way to ask for the Japanese to have a heart and save the dolphins. Unfortunately, we were not welcome there. As soon as we got there we were thrown out. They would not accept our cards and called the police to remove us, when we were willing to leave when they asked. Why? What were we doing that was so offensive? Maybe they feel guilty about the horrible violence their country is committing against these innocent animals. Why else should they be so defensive?

For anyone interested in helping the dolphins, I would suggest researching opportunities to get involved. Educate yourself on what exactly is happening so you can tell your friends and spread the news. The more people know about what is happening to dolphins, the more of a difference we can make. Think of creative, peaceful ways to help give the dolphins a voice to be heard. They deserve it.

Dominic and Aaliyanah were also there with their valentines for the dolphins.

Dominic wrote in his blog that night...

...Susan said "please take these valentine cards for the dolphins" then this guy (consulate representative) got mad. He said "why do you come here every year?! We are never going to stop killing dolphins. We will never stop!" I don't care I'm always going to speak up when something is wrong. What happens to those dolphins and whales is wrong!

Judith Hurst, the founder of the school Anna attends, had this to say after the "Valentines for Dolphins" event:

"I encourage all young people to be informed about all injustices (including those towards animals) and to use their peaceful voices to bring awareness to suffering, in the hopes of revealing hidden brutalities."

 Please visit: dolphinproject.org.

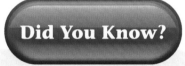

- Fifty percent of all dolphins die within their first two years of captivity.

- Dolphins have saved the lives of humans far back in history. Ancient wall drawings show dolphins leading lost ships away from dangerous rocks.

- The U.S. Navy is conducting experiments in the ocean with high decibel sonar sounds, underwater bomb detonations and gunnery exercises. This will significantly harm marine mammals 9.6 million times between 2013 and 2018. The high-frequency blasts of sound have caused mass deaths of dolphins and other sea life. In human terms the sounds can be thousands of times more powerful than a jet engine. (Source: NRDC Lethal Sounds-Environmental Issues and Public news service, Sept. 27, 2013 Court to Navy: Shhhh! Sonar Disruptive to Sea life. Jan 27, 2014 aldf.org group sues feds)

- Ric O'Barry, the trainer from "Flipper" the TV show, decided to work to release dolphins after the fourth Flipper died in his arms. He's also featured in the Oscar Award Winning documentary movie *The Cove*.

Anna at the Japanese Consulate

Activity Ideas!

- 🐾 Write a letter to the editor of your local newspaper asking people not to support captive dolphin parks, and businesses like swimming with the dolphins.

- 🐾 Make your own letter and art picture and send it to the Japanese consulate in your area asking to please have a heart and stop killing dolphins.

- 🐾 Plan your own Valentine delivery to the Japanese consulate near you. Contact animalherokids.org for support.

Chapter 23

Sharks Need Our Help Too!

13 year old Thomas Ponce Lobbies for All Animals

Don't Just Dream of Change, **LOBBY FOR IT !**
www.LobbyForAnimals.org

When Thomas Ponce was 11 years old he saw a baby shark gasping for air as he lay dying on the deck of a pier. "This shark hasn't lived" pleaded Thomas to the fisherman. A group of onlookers had formed, 20 minutes of pleas later, Thomas finally succeeded and saved the infant shark's life. "I saw a gleam of gratitude in the shark's eye" said Thomas as he returned the creature to his or her ocean home. "I could see first-hand the vulnerability of this beautiful animal and knew how wrong people were in their belief that they were mindless killing machines as Hollywood has so often depicted them."

Thomas, a vegetarian since age 4 and now vegan, is a gifted middle school student. He formed Lobby for Animals to teach people how to effectively lobby to bring about change. Lobby For Animals offers training videos which address the importance of lobbying, speaking at town hall meetings, links to find your legislators, how to make phone calls and write letters to your elected officials along with templates that can be customized, as well as general pointers and tips to help you be more successful in your lobbying efforts.

Thomas received his Animal Hero Kids Kind to All Award at the 2013 Orlando Earth Day Festival. Here's what Thomas said in his acceptance speech; he succeeded in keeping the full attention of the crowd.

"I'd like to start off by saying thank you to Animal Hero Kids for this award. I really appreciate it. I agree and respect their mission of educating people, especially young people on the ways in which they can get involved and help animals. This mission is one that we both share and take an active role in spreading.

Being an advocate and a vegan is all about compassion and making an ethical decision to do as little harm as possible to another living being. It's about speaking up for those who cannot speak up for themselves.

Each time you make the choice of what to eat or wear, which products to buy, whether to attend a circus or a marine park, and which companies you choose to support, you have to realize that your decisions affect more than just you. Remember that there are other lives at stake, the lives of animals, and one life should not be held more valuable than another.

Just because you are not committing the act yourself, doesn't mean it's not happening or that you are not contributing to it. As a consumer if you are not making ethical, cruelty-free choices, you are still fueling the demand. If you do not speak up, buy differently and demand that things be changed you are contributing to the problem.

It takes proactive people to bring about change. People who will take the time to learn about ways in which they can get involved and make a

difference for animals, as well as for the world we live in. The information and resources are out there for whoever wants to learn. I am a firm believer that knowledge is definitely power, and when you speak with knowledge and from your heart, people will listen, regardless of your age.

Lobbying is an excellent way to be proactive. It is essentially reaching out to those involved in introducing and passing our legislation. As citizens we have the opportunity, and, the responsibility to change the future of things, we can make this world a better place for animals and human beings alike by educating ourselves, raising awareness and getting involved in the political process. As citizens, if we speak up and demand that our laws reflect our values, we can create a better world.

It's not difficult to get involved at the legislative level. Start by going online. Just Google any topic you're interested in, let's say vivisection. Learn about the topic, read about what companies are performing the experiments, then, write a letter, or an e-mail, make a phone call, tell them how you feel about it. Research online what bills are being discussed that effect your topic.

Go to my website: www.lobbyforanimals.org to look up who your legislators are, get to know them, and contact them with either your support or to express your opposition. Make an appointment to speak to them about your issue and have your opinion heard. If it's an issue that is not being addressed by legislators currently, **address it!** They will listen to you, it's their job. There are plenty of bills that have been passed into law that were initiated by citizens. The key is to be well informed, prepared and persistent, don't ever give up.

I welcome any of you who want to learn about living a cruelty-free, compassionate life, lobbying and becoming more active in the fight for animal rights as well as our planet to contact me and I would be more than happy to help you in any way I can.

My hope is that one day we will live in a world where awarding people for their compassion and kindness will be an unnecessary act because it will just be a way of life.

Thank you very much for this award and for the opportunity to speak with you all here today. Remember, check out my website, e-mail me, and don't just dream of change... lobby for it!"

One of the goals Thomas has is to ban the sale, distribution, possession, and trade of shark fins and shark fin products in Florida. He hopes to cut off the demand for shark fins and help preserve the species. Thomas wrote a bill that gained support from the Senate and House of Representatives; it did not make it through the entire legislative process. This does not daunt Thomas and he won't give up. He believes the quote on his site from Martin Luther King, *"Our life begins to end the moment we remain silent about things that matter."*

Thomas also created a club in his school to address a variety of animal and compassionate living issues called Harley's Home. Here are his tips to start your own school club.

Thomas' 3 Steps To Starting a School Club

Formulate a plan: *Figure out what you want your club to be about and what specific issues you want to address. Write your syllabus and a month's worth of curriculum (at least). Figure out a supply list for any projects you have planned and think about your budget and any fundraising opportunities you can put together to help pay for your supplies.*

Gathering support: *Start talking to people and set up a sign-up sheet for anyone who might be interested in becoming a member or volunteering with your club. If you can show an interest from other students it is a great selling point to use when speaking to your administrators. Speak to some of your teachers who you think might be willing to sponsor you (if that is a requirement at your school). Make sure it is someone who shares your vision.*

The pitch: *Gather all your information in a presentation. Use PowerPoint to introduce your club idea to your Principal/Dean/Guidance Counselor. Express in your presentation why your club is important and what need it will fill, i.e., raising awareness, promoting compassion, encouraging proactive behavior, and leadership skills. Make an appointment to speak to your administrators. Arrive for your appointment on time and dress for success. All that's left is to make your pitch!*

Good luck and if anyone needs any help I am always available to help whoever I can. Just e-mail me or contact me on Facebook.

Thank you,
Thomas

Did You Know?

🐾 There is no age restriction to make an appointment to see an elected official or to speak at city, county, or state commission meetings.

🐾 Animal Hero Kids Co-Presidents Aaliyanah and Dominic were both under 9 when they spoke to city commissioners to ban electro shock prods being used in the city of Miramar and Margate in Florida. This effectively stops circuses from doing shows in the area.

🐾 Most states have a felony animal cruelty law in place. If it can be proven a person intentionally meant to cause suffering to an animal, they can be charged with felony animal cruelty. Animal research facilities can be exempt from animal cruelty laws.

🐾 Undercover video footage of animals being harmed has helped change laws in industries that use animals and helped convict animal abusers.

🐾 The Animal Legal Defense Fund and People for the Ethical Treatment of Animals have filed the nation's first lawsuit in Utah for limiting the rights of free speech of activists, investigators, and journalists in making it a criminal offence to document cruelty.

🐾 There are over 440 species of sharks.

Activity Ideas!

🐾 Discover on the Lobby for Animals and Animal Legal Defense Fund websites what bills and legal cases are currently in need of letter-writing support. Split the class into groups. Each group chooses a case for which they wish to write letters. They then read their letters to the class.

🐾 Find the endangered species list of sharks and what can be done to help them.

🐾 Research how to cut down on plastic in your home. So much plastic ends up in the ocean. Many marine mammals suffocate after ingesting plastic bags and other plastic garbage.

lobbyforanimals.org

aldf.org (Animal Legal Defense Fund)

sharkfreemarina.org (Shark Free Marina Campaign)

sharksavers.org

shark4kids.com

Chapter 24

Elephants Never Forget...

I met my first elephant being used in a circus two decades ago. This elephant was being led in the hot sun giving kids a ride on her back, and I saw the grey powder that was covering her old injuries, near a wound on her upper chest area. As I watched the man who worked for the circus touched the elephant's wound with a small, inoffensive looking black stick with a box on the end. This was a transistorized electro shock prod. I called the police and reported this. Surely this was animal cruelty? Then I found out all circuses use electro shock prods. Where electro shock prods are banned, circuses with animals no longer visit.

I first heard about this amazing Animal Hero Teen from my friend and elephant capture undercover videographer, filmmaker, Tim Gorski. Tim captured Juliette's lifesaving adventure in his documentary film "How I Became an Elephant".

Juliette was 14 years old when, after saving and fundraising for her quest, she realized her dream of rescuing an elephant. In Thailand, there was a female elephant who was chained all the time, and used by the elephant tourist industry to breed other elephants. The elephant's legs and feet were injured from the constant chaining and abuse. She led a miserable life, like so many elephants used in the entertainment and tourist industry all over the world.

Juliette's dad accompanied Juliette on her journey to Thailand. When they arrived in Thailand they were saddened by the condition of elephants being used by their handlers called "Mahouts" by locals. The elephants are used to beg in the city streets at night outside busy bars and in traffic. So many elephants were thin and had injuries where their chains and ropes were constantly cutting into their flesh. Juliette knew that many elephants escaped their captivity and broke away from their chains when they sensed an impending tsunami.

Tim introduced Juliette to Lek, the woman who ran an elephant sanctuary in Thailand called Elephant Nature Park. Juliette marveled at the gentle nature of the largest land mammal, even after they were harmed by humans, they still had a peaceful, stillness about them.

The founder of the sanctuary knew about the elephant that Juliette had fundraised to afford to buy her away from her life of slavery.

Lek and Juliette set out to see the elephant. Tim filmed as Lek began to negotiate, diplomatically, for the elephant's release. A deal was finally made and transportation arranged with a large truck. It was dark when the entourage arrived, slowly, the elephant walked down the ramp, using her trunk to sniff the new surroundings. Her feet were causing her considerable pain. Lek tended to her sores and placed her arms around her and sang a soothing lullaby to comfort her.

Lek from Elephant Nature Park Sanctuary sings a lullaby to rescued elephant

Juliette's dream saved this one elephant and began her on the path to continue to save more. In 2012, I presented Juliette with the Ricky Williams Animal Hero Teen Award named after the Heisman trophy winner and former NFL star at the Fort Lauderdale Film Festival. A group of 175 students watched on the big screen via a Skype call from California as Juliette received her award.

191

Juliette soothes a victim of the tourist trade, an orphaned baby elephant at Elephant Nature Park Sanctuary, in Thailand.

Today Juliette continues her dream of helping all elephants by booking speaking engagements in schools, and events and mentoring others in becoming leaders. Juliette's goal is to raise people's awareness about what goes on behind the scenes at circuses and within the ivory trade, so that we can put an end to the mistreatment of these animals. She feels especially passionate about raising awareness among young people and hopes that many of the young people whom she reaches will become youth leaders themselves.

See more at:
http://juliettespeaks.org/about/juliette-west/#sthash.0gH3oMRV.dpuf
rattlethecage.org
howibecameanelephant.com
ears.org
elephantnaturepark.org

Celia at Elephant Nature Park

ears.org

Celia, the Elephant Girl

The Russell Simmons Creative Animal Hero Kids Award Song Category winner went to a 14 year old girl living in China in 2013. Celia wrote the song lyrics from the viewpoint of a mother elephant who was talking to her baby and to poachers. Celia's song, called "This Ache" went straight to the heart of the elephant poaching issue.

Elephant Nature Park helps abused victims of Thailand's' tourist industry.
ears.org

Celia, a teen who has teamed up with 40 schools to stop the sale of ivory in China, earned the nickname the "Elephant Girl" from chimpanzee expert, Jane Goodall. Here's her story...

"I am Celia. I started to be interested in elephants when I first read the cover story "Blood Ivory" written by Bryan Christy in *National Geographic*. It inspired me a lot and I have also comprehended the troubles elephants are facing. For the sake of satisfying the limitless hunger of ivory collectors, at least 25,000 to 35,000 elephants are killed every year. Picture the scene. Smell the death. It's cruel and inhumane.

Not only elephants are suffering, but also humans. Some of the money made from selling ivory is then used to purchase weapons used in the continent's various conflicts. Besides, many courageous rangers are killed every year when defending elephants and rhinos. Too many lives have been paying for the ivory trade.

Elephants are important to forest regeneration and creating habitats for many animals when they disperse seeds by eating fruit. Therefore, poaching elephants affects the eco-system.

These were why I started my campaign to help them get out of this inhuman trench and inspire others to protect elephants with essays, songs, videos, and public speech. With people united, we can save elephants from the bloody poaching.

There are basically three parts of my campaign. The first part is drawing ivory consumers' attention so that the demand for ivory can be reduced. And the second part is educating young people, especially in China, because they have the greatest possibility to become future ivory consumers. The last part is drawing international attention to this ivory trade issue.

Everyone has his or her power, which is very influential. They can make good use of their social network, by maybe writing a status on Facebook or sending a letter to newspapers, just like I have done. They can also educate people around them and their parents, because they all have the possibility to become ivory consumers. Young people's voices can be heard easily, and they are always noticed by others.

Tell people around you not to buy ivory.

The supply of ivory is no longer sustainable. It is time for us to rectify our mistakes before an irreversible disaster occurs. Please stop devastating a species that is already losing ground. Before they become extinct, let's save them, and our planet as well."

"This Ache"

Roaming through the woodlands
Feeling the soft sunlight
Dreaming of those days

Loving you my child
And I'll be watching over you
Though my end comes nearer

They're coming with their big guns
Grim looks with their cold eyes
Ready for a bloodshed

Run 'way for your life child
Get 'way from my side now
My love alone will stand and last

Why're we suffering this ache?

1st Chorus
I cried, I begged, you still go on
Bullets one by one
Hefty dose of grief
Parting tears are all over my face
Have you ever cried one drop for me?
Think of all your loved ones, wake up, wake up!
Set me free!
You faces are impassive over blood
Only for those useless so-called art
You'll get nothing but a prove of killing
So what's the point,
Of buying these?

Humming a lullaby
Kissing the pale moonlight
Dreaming of those nights

Missing you my child
Like the stars missing the sun
In the morning sky

They're getting my tusks out
Holding bloody hands up
Putting their lives at risks as well

Close your weeping eyes child
Flaming pool's beside now
Mom's no longer beautiful
Why're we suffering this ache?

1st Chorus again

2nd Chorus
I prayed, I dreamed, to stop this ache
Holding my child tight
We'll be like those days
When we would whisper in the breeze
Glorify how wondrous bird songs were
Remember how the bees lured us to find where
Flowers were
When you would hook my trunk with a goodnight kiss
Velvet moonlight sought and found us still
Remember how I sang you my slumber-song
Till your eyelids weighed
Can't this be real?

Source: Lyrics and vocals by Celia Ho Yen Kei Melody from 'Video Games', by Lana Del Rey and Justin Parker http://juliettespeaks.org/beautiful-song-from-elephant-mama-to-elephant-baby/

A Message from Arielle, Animal Hero Kids Co-Pres

Circuses harm and exploit animals for entertainment. Circuses steal docile creatures like elephants away from their families and use bull hooks to force them to perform cruel and unnatural tricks. Circuses are wrong because they deprive animals of freedom and the ability to interact with their families and be out in the wild where they belong. Animals in circuses live lonely, isolated lives on the road in dark boxcars and cages.

Elephants live in chains and are unable to travel the hundreds of miles they do out in the wild foraging for food and interacting in social groups. Elephants and tigers and other animals in circuses are whipped and beaten in order to make them perform unnatural and silly tricks. Their spirits are broken when they are babies during harsh training sessions so they fear their trainers and submit to their commands. Circuses are no fun for animals.

I received an Animal Hero Kids Award for a school video project I did in middle school educating my peers about circus cruelty. For my television production class, I had to make a video about an issue the government should change. I made my video about why the government should ban circuses, especially the Ringling Brothers Circus.

In the video, I filmed myself and other protesters outside of the Amway Center in Orlando protesting against the Ringling Bros. Circus when it came into town. I also included videos of animals in the circus being whipped and abused by their trainers. I played this video to the whole school and I changed several of my fellow students' and teachers' minds about the circus. One teacher personally came up to me and told me she would never go to the circus again after watching the video I created.

I'm proud to stand with Animal Hero Kids, a non-profit organization, which offers free humane education programs in schools and recognizes children and youth who go above and beyond to help all species of animals in need. I believe the same as Animal Hero Kids that teaching children and youth to be compassionate toward all beings is the key to preventing animals being harmed in the future. I really like when we give awards to kids of all ages who show extraordinary acts of kindness toward animals.

As co-president of Animal Hero Kids, I do a lot of speaking and volunteering at events, including at award shows and festivals to educate people about the organization and being kind to animals. I gave a speech recently in my college speech class about why people should go vegan and talked about the enormous suffering farmed animals endure in the meat and dairy industry. As co-president, I help promote Animal Hero Kids and recruit youth to join this amazing, inspiring organization. As co-president, I also serve as a role model and ambassador for all species of animals and aim to inspire children and teens to be kind to all animals and volunteer to help them.

Wisdom to Help Elephants

Kane, 13, and Donavon, 9, help animals every day by being vegan. They like to protest the circus and have an important message for you.
Two siblings share their message of compassion...

13 year old Kane says:
Animals in the circus are whipped and beaten with a bull hook until they are so scared and hurt that they will do what the trainer says. It's wrong to harm animals. It's just like hurting a person. They have feelings and family and are intelligent, too. The best thing to do to help animals is to try gradually working up to eating a plant-based diet and refrain from activities that involve animals such as, circuses, zoos, sea world, pony rides, petting zoos, etc.

9 year old Donavon says:
The animals get beaten up in the circus. It's wrong; the animals don't do anything to us. You can stop going to circuses and zoos and eat vegan to help animals that are hurt."

Sunder, the rescued elephant

More than 220,000 people around the world wrote to authorities seeking Sunder, an abused elephant's release through action alerts on PETA affiliates' websites. Many celebrities, including Paul McCartney and Pamela Anderson, took to Twitter or wrote letters to keep the spotlight on Sunder's plight. PETA India's lawyers argued well, its veterinarians and experts were invaluable, and the Animal Rahat (PETA India) staff endured many sleepless nights and risked bodily harm in the face of interference and near rioting by those who fought to keep Sunder from freedom. Sunder is still recovering from a massive leg injury caused by long-term confinement to tight, heavy chains, so she has not yet been permitted to walk freely through the park with the rest of the elephants, but she's allowed to mingle with them when they're in a smaller area, and as soon as her leg heals, she'll have free run of the park's 122 acres of forests, streams, and ponds.

Did You Know?

- Elephants travel up to 100 miles a day in the wild with their extended family.

- An elephant who was rescued thanks to the work of PETA, recently named Sunder called out to all the other elephants when she arrived at the sanctuary at night.

- Elephants live in matriarchal societies.

- A former animal trainer, Pat Derby, saw such animal cruelty in circuses she opened a sanctuary and began rescuing the animals instead.

- Tons of ivory was destroyed by the Hong Kong government to help stop the ivory trade.

- It is not legal to have captive wildlife perform in circuses in the United Kingdom.

- Today, most zoos are sad places for animals. They are simply museums of living beings kept in cement pens or small outdoor enclosures. Although they get basic food and water, they don't have much to do and are bored. Elephants and other wild animals kept captive develop a constant weaving back and forth. This is called stereotypical behavior. The longer the elephants are kept captive the more they move their head from side to side.

- The *Antiques Roadshow* TV show decided to no longer feature ivory on their program.

Activity Ideas!

☙ If a circus is coming to town, write a letter to the editor explaining the cruelty involved in the training, transportation, and caging or chaining of these animals. When tickets stop selling for animal abusive entertainment, the incentive to cage and chain them will be gone.

☙ Organize a protest; follow Dominic's tips on organizing a protest in Chapter 21.

☙ Do a school presentation about the state of elephants and what everyone can do to help. Animal Hero Kids has a free DVD for your school about helping all animals with a segment about circuses. Teachkind.org and peta2.com can also help with free materials about circuses.

☙ As a birthday or holiday gift, help sponsor an elephant on behalf of a friend or relative. Find out about ways to sponsor or "adopt" an animal by providing the costs of their care and other costs at http://www.animalrahat.com/.

☙ The Elephant Sanctuary in Hohenwald, Tennessee, is a 2,700 acre respite for former circus and zoo elephants. There are virtual "visits" for classrooms or groups anywhere in the world, where students have the opportunity to learn about rescued elephants living in the United States largest natural habitat for Asian and African elephants. The non-intrusive fourteen digital, solar powered ele-cams located throughout the habitats, make it possible to see the elephants who reside at the Elephant Sanctuary. www.elephants.com.

Chapter 25

Hannah Rallies for Rhinos

"I am an 11 year old middle school student. In addition to being a regular kid who loves art, soccer and her friends, I have always been passionate about animals. I have also been very passionate about the environment, particularly in environmental topics that have an impact on animals. As far back as kindergarten I have educated students on various environmental topics.

I stepped up my efforts in the last two years and have become a voice for those that do not have a voice. I recognized I could have more of an impact if I teamed up with other organizations, and I have gotten involved in organizations such as One More Generation, SaveTheHorses, WildAid, Keep Forsyth Beautiful, Keep Bermuda Beautiful, Greening Forward, and the Plastic Pollution Coalition. I wanted to share my story so you could see that anyone at any age can make a difference in this world. Everything I have

Hannah (center) with rhino friends

Creating Elvis and getting him ready for the world to see was a lot of hard work but so worth it

done has been rather easy to accomplish, and with the support of my family and friends I have been able to make a difference in a short period of time.

I found on the Internet an Atlanta non-profit, One More Generation (OMG) that was helping to raise awareness of the plight of rhinos in South Africa. Black rhinos are being killed for their horns, and they are on the endangered list as there are only a few left in the world. I decided to raise awareness in my own little way by holding an event at our home. I thought instead of a lemonade stand, I would have an "awareness stand" and invite everyone we knew. My parents and I placed posters around town and emailed our friends. In just 3 short days, we held a very successful event outside of our house which was attended by over 200 people.

After this event, I traveled to Virginia and spoke to about 80 children and 70 adults about rhinos. I asked my relatives for help too, and my grandparents in England spread the word and helped collect petitions. After a couple of months, I obtained over 1,700 signed petitions and letters from around the world for OMG to present to South Africa's government leaders. In addition, due to my passion and commitment, my elementary school and OMG got involved and we made one of the largest paper-mache rhinos in the world. Elvis the Rhino was featured in Hartsfield-Jackson International Airport, which is a busy airport, to raise awareness of this issue. All in all, I touched thousands of people who had no idea rhinos were being senselessly killed, and hopefully my actions and those of OMG will help persuade the South African government to take action to protect the rhinos. If you want to get involved, it is easy to write a letter to show the South African government that you care about their animals.

A few years ago I found an organization online called The David Sheldrick Wildlife Trust that is based in Kenya and takes care of elephants and rhinos that are orphaned from their parents. It is so sad that these animals are being killed for their tusks and horns. For several years I have fostered elephants and rhinos. At every holiday season, one of my gifts is a fostered animal from this amazing organization. You can do this too! Just think about it, you could be living far from Kenya, but you could be helping animals across the globe! If you love these animals, tell your parents you want to help foster one. You can even tell your friends to get them involved! It is so simple to foster an animal from this organization or other ones. For every animal I foster, the money goes to take care of the animals and I receive a certificate and a monthly update on the animal's life. I have spread the word about this organization to many friends at school, and many of them have also sponsored an animal themselves.

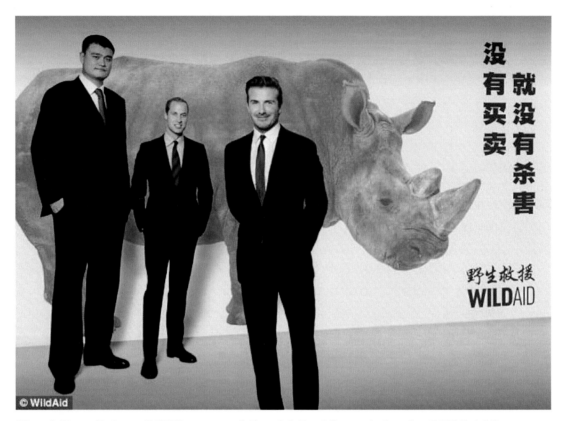

没有买卖 就没有杀害

野生救援
WILDAID

*Yao Ming, Prince William, and David Beckham join the Wild Aid
Campaign for rhinos.*

As you can hopefully tell from my story, you are never too young to make
a difference. You just have to believe in something, and be passionate about
it, and maybe even a little creative. Keep in mind that being a child has its
advantages! You can easily relate to other kids, and even adults will listen
because they are usually so surprised a child is speaking about a worldly
topic! I found that teaming up with others that share in your vision also
helps a lot. We all live on the same earth, and we can all make a difference
in our own little way. Give it a try, start small and you may be surprised at
how you can make a difference in this world.

I am not entirely sure where all of this will take me and what I might accomplish next. I just know that I continue to love animals and plan to find other opportunities to help those that don't have a voice.

As Gandhi would say, "You must be the change you wish to see in the world." And I am trying my best to make a difference in my own little way. I may be only one person with one voice, but together we can make a wave to help our world. I hope I have inspired you to be the change!"

The greatness of a nation and its moral progress can be judged by the way its animals are treated. – Mahatma Gandhi

Did You Know?

- There are five species of rhinoceros: two African and three Asian. The African species are the white and black rhinos. Both species have two horns. Asian rhinos include the Indian and the Javan, each with one horn, and the Sumatran, which has two horns.

- The white rhino is the second largest land mammal next to the elephant. The five species of rhino weigh anywhere from 750 pounds to 8,000 pounds.

- Many famous people have joined the campaign for rhinos including Chinese basketball star, Yao Ming, England's Prince William, and British soccer star David Beckham.

- White rhinos live in the savanna and black rhinos like in dense forests in tropical and subtropical regions.

- Rhinos can run up to 28 miles per hour.

Activity Ideas!

- ❧ Discover on the wildaid.org site what they are doing to help rhinos.

- ❧ Animal People News is a respected chronicle of animal issues. Research on their site what the salaries and direct-mail marketing costs are of the animal protection groups. Conclude with a percentage of how much money goes to direct animal help or salaries or direct-mail marketing.

- ❧ Charity Navigator is another way to check out charities before donating.

Yazamean (Yazi) and Aaliyanah

Chapter 26

Lions, Tigers, and Bears... Oh My!

Ali Roars for Lions and Tigers

Aaliyanah, Animal Hero Kids co-president educates about captive animals in the circus at protests and city commission meetings. Animal Hero Kids Humane Education complimentary school presentations educate about helping wild animals stay wild, including tigers. Interactive dramatizations where the children dress up as the animals in the wild help to create an understanding of wild animals' natural homes and their family life.

When a group of Grade 4 students in Philadelphia realized how much room tigers in the circus have in the cages they spend most of their life in, they were shocked. The three students asked their school principal if they could create a cage in their school hallway to sit in, for other students to consider the daily reality of confined animals. The principal consented; the three boys sat in the cage they had made with a sign telling the facts about the life captive tigers lead. The whole school population learned about the reasons not to support the use of captive wildlife in the entertainment industry.

Paul Hines, teacher at Springside Chestnut Hill Academy, PA, Carlo Filippini, Alex Johnson, Sante Filippini educating about the size of cages for tigers after a 22reasons.org presentation.

Joe is 13 years old and has a Facebook page called Roars and Trumpets. He shares news and raises awareness for animals around the world, with a focus on elephants and tigers kept in captivity and exploited. He gathers film footage and photos of facilities that keep captive tigers and asks people not to support jailing wildlife.

One of Aaliyanah's favorite places to visit on the web is Performing Animal Welfare Society's website where she reads about their three sanctuaries caring for 100 wild animals rescued from zoos, circuses, and individuals who tried to make pets out of wild animals.

Rescued lions at a wildlife sanctuary

Bolivia banned wild animals used in circuses as did India, Peru, Austria, and the United Kingdom. Animal Defenders International and Performing Animal Welfare Society (PAWS) joined forces to give sanctuary to the last lions used in circuses by transporting the lions to their Galt, California sanctuary. Bob Barker, the former *Price is Right* host and Jorja Fox, from *CSI* assisted with the mission. An award winning movie was made about the lion's journey called *The Lion Ark.*

Animal Hero Kids and Susan Hargreaves with Pamela Anderson, who has had a lifelong commitment to helping animals

215

Animal Hero Kids young volunteers performed a spoken word poem for Pamela Anderson, actress and Ingrid Newkirk, activist, for their birthday celebration called, "We're All Animals". Here's the tiger verse.

We're All Animals

Like a tiger in his cage,

He looks up to the sky,

He longs to be free,

We feel his sad rage,

We're All Animals

How can we help them ?

You and Me

How can we help our animal family?

First, we can do no harm,

Yes, Do no harm,

that rule, works like a charm

and remember...

We're all Animals

Can't you see

We're all Animals

part of the same family

We're all Animals

http://www.ad-international.org/adi_home/
http://www.pawsweb.org/meet_tigers.html

Animals should be free to live their lives and enjoy their natural homes.
– tweeted Pamela Anderson

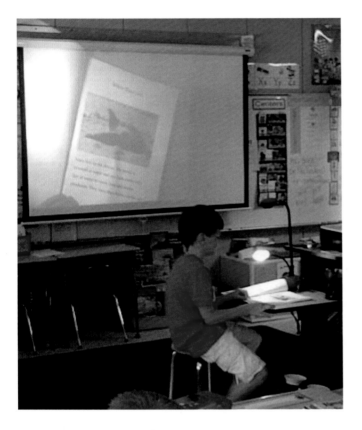

"Jails, No Picnic for Bears"

Eleven-year-old, Animal Hero Kids co-president, Dominic, helps all animals. He's a vegan animal activist who protests any animal abusive practices and does school presentations about helping animals any chance he gets. One school project was about how to help bears. Dominic was following and cheering on a recent bear rescue, helped by Sam Simon, "The Simpsons" Co-Creator, PETA, Wild Animal Sanctuary and the Atlanta Humane Society.

Seventeen bears were in a zoo in Helen, Georgia, in concrete pits, were they led lonely, unnatural lives without ever feeling grass under their paws or running in the open air or knowing what it was like to climb a tree. The two female bears, Ursula and O.B., had their baby cubs sold away from them, again and again, crying and being held back each time; a common occurrence in zoos and circuses where they trade and sell animals.

Then the animal rescue collaborative team stepped in. The move to a 60 acre habitat utilized climate controlled trailers, emergency locations were set up on the route to Colorado, just in case any of the bears got sick on the way. No stops were needed as the bears seemed to enjoy the ride and discovering new healthy foods as they traveled.

217

When the bears first arrived at the sanctuary, the rescue team opened the trailer doors and let the bears slowly look around at their new surroundings before moving them into their new habitat. One adult brown bear, Dakota, immediately stepped out of the cage, put his nose to the ground, and started smelling and exploring the environment and then he started to graze. It didn't take long before he was running joyously and incredulously around his new vast home.

The bears are now at the Wild Animal Sanctuary. They live in spacious, species-specific habitats with the freedom to roam, nest, forage, and enjoy fresh fruits and vegetables. Ursula and O.B. were pregnant before they left the zoo. Their baby cubs were born in the 60 acre sanctuary. This is the first time their babies were not taken away. Dominic says, "The rescued bears went from being in a cement pit begging for scraps from tourists to being in a wild Colorado picnic paradise."

A rescued bear feels grass under his paws for the first time thanks to PETA

Did You Know?

- 🐾 It is now illegal for wild animals to be captured, transported, and displayed in circuses in India, Peru, Austria, and the United Kingdom.

- 🐾 Tigers and lions are still used in traveling shows, circuses, and zoos in the United States.

- 🐾 The domestic cat is descended from wild big cats and still shares a lot of the same movements and behaviors.

- 🐾 Lions defend their territory, which they have marked by spraying urine or rubbing their scent on trees and bushes around the perimeter. It is the sole responsibility of the males to defend the pride against invading males and this is done by using their magnificent manes and roars to intimidate potential rivals, thus, to an extent, avoiding potentially dangerous and sometimes fatal direct conflict.

In this year's National Animal Rights Day (NARD) event, Genesis read the Declaration of Animal Rights with her friend, Joseph. They are both young, vegan animal rights activists. The two did an amazing job and I am sure they will continue to work together to help all animals!

219

Did You Know?

🐾 Prides can include up to three males, around a dozen females, and their young, which are raised cooperatively after they reach 6-8 weeks old, when they are first introduced to the pride. All of the lionesses in the pride will be related to one another and the female cubs typically stay with the group for life. Young males on the other hand leave the pride and seek to establish a pride of their own by driving out existing pride males.

🐾 The actress from the movie *Born Free*, Virginia McKenna, began a Zoocheck campaign in 1984 and created the Born Free Foundation.

🐾 Some zoos sell surplus animals to canned hunt operations and roadside zoos. Canned hunts are where the animal is shot in a fenced area.

🐾 The last remaining lions used in entertainment in Bolivia were transported to PAWS Sanctuary through a partnership of two charities. Their lifelong care is funded by Animal Defenders International. The lions are now in a 22 acre habitat at Performing Animal Welfare Society's sanctuary.

🐾 Lions, tigers, and bears are all mammals like humans.

Activity Ideas!

🐾 Go to pawsweb.org to research how to "adopt" a tiger. That means to pay for care, medical expenses... for one year of a tiger saved.

🐾 Have a vegan party with your friends and watch the uplifting movie *The Lion Ark*. Go to lionarkthemovie.com for details and learn how to help the last remaining lions in Peru.

🐾 Measure a space the size of a lion or tiger's cage. Create your own "cage" like the boys in this chapter. Create fact cards about lions and tigers in captivity to display on your cage.

🐾 Animal People News is a respected source for animal issues. Research on their website what the salaries and direct mail marketing costs are of the animal protection groups. Conclude with a percentage of how much money goes to direct animal help versus salaries or direct mail marketing.

🐾 Charity Navigator is another way to check out charities before donating.

🐾 Organize a protest if a circus is coming to your town, or contact city commissioners to ask for a ban on exotic performing animal acts. Contact peta2kids.com, animalherokids.org, animaldefendersinternational.org and pawsweb.org for advice.

🐾 Go to zoocheck.org to download the activities for your grade level.

🐾 Be a whistleblower, call: 1-866-966-8477, 1-866-ZOO-TIPS.

🐾 wildanimalsanctuary.org

Chapter 27

"We are all Primates"

Monica Naranjo from Save the Chimps, a sanctuary for chimps who were used in animal experiments told me about 14 year old Brandon. When Brandon found out about chimpanzees being harmed in research laboratories, zoos, and circuses, he decided to do something about it. This actually turned into quite a few things. I'll let Brandon tell you all about it.

He began by creating his own website called "Make a Chimp Smile" because he loves all animals but Great Apes are his favorite. His goal through Make a Chimp Smile is to help raise funds for Great Ape sanctuaries. Brandon is a great volunteer and supporter of Save the Chimps, the largest chimp sanctuary in the world. Coulston Laboratories, an animal research company with the most number of animal welfare violations was notorious for being cruel. Save the Chimps founder, Dr. Carole Noon, bought the failing research company and gradually introduced the Coulston lab chimps to a nature-filled, group existence on eight islands. Here's Brandon's message...

"When I was nine years old I really wanted to have a chimp as a pet but, after doing research, I learned how wrong it was to keep a chimpanzee as a pet. During my research I learned about Save the Chimps Sanctuary. They were rescuing chimpanzees from a lab in New Mexico and bringing them to the sanctuary in Fort Pierce, Florida. There was one chimp named Elway who is around my age and he was already at the Sanctuary but his father whose name was Boy was still in New Mexico. I thought that maybe since I couldn't have a chimp as a pet that maybe I could help one. This is when I started fundraising for Save the Chimps to help bring Boy to Florida.

The more I learned about chimpanzees and other great apes and what they have gone through and how much they are like humans is amazing. I don't think many people think or know about the suffering chimpanzees have gone through. Chimpanzees are our closest living relatives. They share the same emotions as we do and are like us in so many ways. Baby chimps depend on their mothers and chimpanzees need to live in family groups. It just isn't right to use them in experiments, keep them as pets, or use them in entertainment.

Chimps in the World Today

Chimpanzees have been getting more attention this past year. The Federal government has been phasing out the use of federally owned chimps in medical research. There are still many chimps that are privately owned but recently a big pharmaceutical company, Merck, announced that they would no longer fund chimpanzees in medical research.

This announcement was big and I hope that all the pharmaceutical companies that still use chimps will do the same. People need to know chimpanzees can live long lives, at least 50 years, and they will need special care when they leave the labs. Also chimps that are used in entertainment are only used up to the age of six. These are the years that they should really be with

their mothers. After the age of six, chimpanzees become too big and too hard to handle. When this happens chimps as well as orangutans are usually sold to a lab, end up locked up in a cage in isolation, or end up in some roadside zoo.

The first thing I did to help chimps was to start a blog with some help from my family. I wrote about the chimpanzees at Save the Chimps and asked people to help out with donations. People started to follow my blog and share it with others on the Internet. I also started tabling events to raise awareness and collect donations. I've had many petitions going over the past couple of years and have written many letters to congress and representatives. Now I have a Facebook and Twitter accounts where I can share information and make more people aware of the plight of the great apes.

Everyone can all help to raise awareness of great apes in labs all they have gone through. They could have fundraisers to help a sanctuary. The chimpanzees and other great apes in Sanctuaries need all kinds of things such as housing, veterinary care, fresh fruit, and nesting blankets.

I don't think anyone is too young to help. All you need to do is come up with an idea. You can also get your friends and family involved. You can make things and sell them to help raise money. I sell lots of things at events

like friendship bracelets, soap, tote bags, and magnets. Or you can make a public service announcement to raise awareness and share it on social media. Right now a big issue is the palm oil plantations in Indonesia. These plantations are destroying our rainforests and killing off our wildlife. The orangutans are in great danger now.

If you believe in something and you know it is right you shouldn't let anyone else bother you. I know it can be hard but you never know, you might just inspire someone else to want to help animals."

Brandon has raised lots of funds for sanctuaries and informs the public about how they can help chimps at his info booths around Florida. Brandon went from asking for a chimpanzee as a pet to really helping chimpanzees stay safe and live free or in a real sanctuary. That's what I call a friend who can truly make a chimp smile. makeachimpsmile.com

My love for animals started when I was a young girl in England. When I grew up all I wanted to do was go to Africa, live with animals, and write books about them. Thanks to my supportive mother, I succeeded in living my dream. My advice would be as my mother told me, "You must work hard, take advantage of opportunities and, above all, never give up."

-Jane Goodall

Madison and Rhiannon: Orangutan Allies

Madison Vorva and Rhiannon Tomtishen met when they went to elementary school. Together they co-founded Project ORANGS, a campaign whose mission is to promote the need for rainforest-safe Girl Scout Cookies and deforestation-free sources of palm oil. The two best friends are passionate about showing consumers that their everyday purchases have global impacts. Madison enjoys sharing her tools for advocacy success with other young people in her presentation "Change Starts with a Passion." Recently, the United Nations honored Madison as a "North American Forest Hero."

Here's Madison's message...

When I was 11 years old, I discovered pictures of dead orangutans who had been beaten, burned and shot after entering palm oil plantations in search of food. After realizing the full magnitude of the situation (50% of the products in our grocery stores contain palm oil) and the true hopelessness that this incredible species is facing, I turned my outrage into unrelenting action.

Here's Rhiannon's message...

As 11 year olds, Madison and I set out to earn our Girl Scout Bronze Award and, inspired by our hero Dr. Jane Goodall's work with the chimpanzees, decided to focus our efforts on raising awareness about the endangered orangutan. We quickly discovered that their rainforest habitat was being destroyed for palm oil production and that this ingredient is in hundreds of the products we consume every day, including Girl Scout cookies. I

was shocked when I found out about the connection between our own organization and these social and environmental issues because through Girl Scouting I had learned environmental stewardship, in fact part of the Girl Scout Law includes "to make the world a better place"!

Madison and I set out to raise awareness on this issue and encourage our organization to adopt a deforestation-free palm oil policy. After five years, support from hundreds of thousands of girls and consumers, and appearances in national media outlets from the Wall Street Journal to NPR to ABC World News, the two of us were finally able to meet with Girl Scout executives and they announced a palm oil policy six months later in 2011, a huge step in the right direction but it does not yet do enough to ensure that all Girl Scout cookies are forest-friendly.

Although the Girl Scouts' policy is not yet strong enough, in February of this year Kellogg's (one of the two bakers of Girl Scout cookies) announced

A rescued laboratory monkey is out of a cage and in a natural environment for the first time. Jungle Friends is a sanctuary with 120 monkeys who have been rescued from the pet, entertainment, or research industries.

a deforestation-free palm oil policy that was the first of its kind for any American company. This policy applies to all of the cookies baked by Little Brownie Bakers (owned by Kellogg's) but the other half of the cookies, produced by ABC Bakers, still aren't forest-friendly. To take a stand on this issue, write to Girl Scouts USA and ABC Bakers to urge them to adopt a truly deforestation-free policy, like the one Kellogg's already has, because deforestation and human rights abuses have no place in Girl Scout cookies!

Both Madison and Rhiannon believe that regardless of your age, gender, or background, we all have the power to make our voices heard and change the world. In an award acceptance speech they said, "We began this project when we were only 11 years old and with passion and hard work have grown it to an international platform; by starting small and dreaming big, you can do the same. As youth, we have the luxury of imagining a vision that appears irrational and can dream in a way that is not limited by an adult's perspective."

Madison has a website teaching about how to create change and she is also on the board of the National Youth Leadership Council with Roots & Shoots.

The Roots & Shoots National Youth Leadership Council (NYLC) is the youth voice of the Jane Goodall Institute (JGI). This group of high school and college Roots & Shoots members apply and interview to be accepted to a one-year (renewable) term. Throughout their term, they are trained to serve as mentors and experts to the Roots & Shoots network, connecting virtually with members around the globe. They help develop materials and plan campaigns for the organization, and they serve as representatives of JGI at workshops, conferences, and events worldwide.

Did You Know?

- Humans are primates too.

- Jane Goodall was only 17 years old when she traveled to observe chimpanzees in the wild with her mom.

- Scientists at the time didn't believe Jane's discovery that chimps use tools like we do.

- Research facilities are exempted from state felony animal cruelty laws.

- The movie industry still uses chimps and other non-human primates. When the monkey smiles it's actually a signal they feel threatened and unsafe.

- The lethal effects of the palm oil industry (being used as a product ingredient) on non-human primates is still unknown by the general public.

Activity Ideas!

- 🐾 Go to the projectorangs.org to discover which products contain palm oil and where to write letting them know you will not buy their products until that ingredient is replaced.

- 🐾 Go to www.junglefriends.org and see the Stop the Pet Trade activity.

- 🐾 Check out the work of Roots & Shoots and the council Madison is on. http://www.janegoodall.org/programs/rootsandshoots/nylc/bios

- 🐾 Create your own 'A Day in the Life of a Jungle Family' interactive play, and perform for your class. Contact education@animalherokids.org for tips.

- 🐾 Watch the film *Plague Dogs*, *Project X*, *Animal Farm*, or *Watership Down* and discuss the animal rights/welfare issues in each.

Saved from research laboratories. SavetheChimps.org

Chapter 28

Top Turtle Hero Kids

Sea turtles are magical. The loggerhead sea turtle is about the size of a large coffee table. The mother will walk up to the spot on the beach, dig a space and lay her eggs all without even turning her head around to look behind her. I had the privilege to be on the beach one day just as it was getting dark, when this huge queen of a loggerhead turtle laid her eggs nearby. I stayed very still, as frozen as a statue, until she finished her work. The light of the moon leads the just hatched babies towards the water as it reflects on the sea at night; it's as if the moon is calling to the hatchlings, "this way, this way"...

However, human lighting at the beach and on the road, streetlights, all disorients the sea turtle babies and they go onto the road, into storm drains. That's why it's so important if you live or work by the beach to make sure lights are out at night, including street lights. Sometimes you will see the

Teakahlah (Tea) WhiteCloud, age 12, turtle hero

reflective lights on the road by the ocean that are called cat's eyes, they're turtle friendly. Animal Hero Kids have given 7 Extraordinary Animal Hero awards to kids saving sea turtles. The estimate of how many turtles these heroes have saved: about 4,000. One rescuer has saved 700 in one summer holiday.

There are 1,000's of very fortunate turtles out there swimming deep under the waves thanks to the help of these special Animal Hero Kids. They volunteer with Sea Turtle Oversight Protection (STOP). They sit on the beach with a parent at night and watch closely for any nests hatching. This is called "Hatching Out." One young girl, Teakahlah, was only 8 years old, when she helped re-direct 100 turtles in one night! Brother and sis, Aron and Denise, are also a great team and help lots of sea turtle hatchlings go into the ocean when they were all turned around and went towards the lights of a house on the beach instead.

"You are never too young to do anything! I started sea turtle work when I was 3 years old.

I like helping sea turtles, they are really cool. I am part of an organization that goes out on the beach at night and helps the sea turtle hatchlings that are disoriented get to the ocean.

I like to help the environment. It gives so much to us and it's time to give back so we can help our planet!

In all my years of experience, I have learned a lot and now I am going share my experiences with you through tips."

Certificate of Birth

on this 31st day of July in the year 2014

we are happy to announce the birth of:

Animal Hero Kids

a healthy Loggerhead Sea Turtle (Caretta caretta)

which went into the sea happy and free

Hatched from Nest # FT274 in Broward County, Florida.

S.T.O.P.

SeaTurtleOP.org

Tea's Turtle Tips:

1. Fill in any holes and level any mounds.
2. Never leave tents, tables or chairs on the beach because they can block the mother turtle from nesting or she can get caught up in them.
3. If you see a nesting mother always make sure you stay at least 50 feet away from her and are very quiet and still.
4. Never shine any lights on the nesting mother or the sea turtle hatchlings.
5. Never bring any kind of lighting onto the beach.
6. If you live on or near the beach, have your parents install turtle safe lighting.
7. Even if you don't live near the beach, have your parents install wildlife safe lighting to help all wildlife!
8. These lights meet 3 standards: 1st - keep it low to the ground. 2nd - keep it shielded, the shield will direct light down where we need it. 3rd - keep it red & amber, these are wildlife safe colors.
9. When your parents are purchasing new outside lighting, look for the wildlife safe certificate on the package.

These tips will save sea turtles!

Here are some OTHER tips for helping the planet and all its creatures.

1. When there are animals that need help, don't think twice, just help!
2. Find animals in your area that need your help.
3. If you think that there is a problem, write a city official on what the problem is and what you think they can do about it.
4. Get involved in an issue and see what you can do to help.
5. Get your community involved in saving our planet.
6. Plant trees, plants, and shrubs for a habitat for animals plus it will help the environment.
7. Separate garbage from recyclables and reduce your use of plastics.
8. Use plastic alternatives like glass and recycled paper products.
9. Always use recycled paper products so we can save trees.
10. Follow the three R's REDUCE-REUSE-RECYCLE also follow the three P's PLANT-PROTECT-PRESERVE.
11. Plant a native garden with native plants.

THANK YOU for helping the animals and the planet!

Sibling Turtle Savers

The Carney siblings know that only one in 10,000 sea turtles makes it to adulthood. Each summer they volunteer for STOP and anxiously anticipate the baby turtles breaking the sand's surface.

Anna tells why... "...like a kid anticipates Christmas morning, people come up to me, curious as to why a 17-year-old girl is sitting on a bucket in the middle of the night staring at a nest. "What are you doing?" has become an all too familiar question. I explain to my audience that I am working with a program that rescues disoriented sea turtle hatchlings

Throughout the night a wide variety of people ask me questions about these endangered animals, and to all of them I promote sea turtle conservation, explaining how crucial it is to our ecosystem that these animals remain on our planet. These people make the night go by surprisingly fast, and finally the moment we have been waiting for arrives, the sand caves in. A couple of minutes later, the babies poke their heads out of the sand. Then the hatchlings begin to crawl. The majority of the turtles frantically crawl towards the street, and then I confidently direct them towards the water and watch as they swim off.

The feeling that I get whenever I help a sea turtle reach the water is unparalleled to any other experience. Not only has this experience taught me that I alone can make a difference, but also it has taught me the importance of every single creature on our planet. Each animal serves a significant purpose that helps balance our ecosystem. If the sea turtles all die, the coral reef will eventually die as well, and if the coral reef dies, most marine life will cease to exist, which will eventually significantly impact the human race. Although that is an extreme worse case scenario, it reinforces my passion for doing what I can to protect our planet and its inhabitants."

Happy Snappy Day!

Here's a story from the Kool 2B Kind band of brothers you met in Section 2: Tristan, Ronan (twins, 9), and little brother Derrian (7) helped save a snapping turtle north of Toronto, in Ontario, Canada.

Here is a before photo showing how badly Snappy was hurt.

"We were coming home from the driving range in Dundalk, north of Toronto, when, all of a sudden, a car coming from the other direction hit a beautiful large male snapping turtle.

Daddy pulled over and Ronan, Derrian, and I jumped out of the minivan to go see if the turtle was still alive. Its head and around one eye were bleeding badly and one front paw seemed to be crushed and bleeding too. But he was still alive.

Daddy lifted him into the back of our minivan. We moved stuff out of the back to make room for him. He was bleeding a lot. We didn't know if he would make it. We got home in 20 minutes and told Mommy what had happened.

She said: Should we put it out of its misery? It looks pretty bad... But Ronan and I said to call Natie (their aunt) at the Wildlife Centre. (Natie or Nathalie Karvonen is the director of the Toronto Wildlife Centre and an expert on all matters dealing with wild animal care and rescue.)

So Mommy called and Natie said to take photos on our cell phone to e-mail her and that she would call us back to tell us what to do. So we used our cell phone (Daddy's old phone that we just use to take photos and to play with sometimes) and took many photos of Snappy's injuries. Oh yeah, we named him Snappy. And Natie told us he was a boy.

Natie called to say to bring him in to the Wildlife Centre that night. We got back in the minivan and drove with Daddy down to Toronto. We were really worried about Snappy. There was a lot of blood in the back, on the carpet. And he wasn't moving much...

Natie sent us e-mail updates 4 times: 1. (Day 2) he had a skull fracture and an injured paw; 2. (Day 4) the vets at the Toronto Wildlife Centre said he was stabilizing and would make it (snapping turtles are very strong and can partially hide their heads under their shells to protect themselves); 3.

(Day 10) Snappy had been introduced into a shallow pool at the Wildlife Centre and was being fed good quality snapping turtle food. I will let Ronan tell you the rest."

"Hi! E-mail number 4 (Day 30) from Natie said that Snappy was all better and could be released in a day or two. Derrian, Tristan, Daddy, Mommy, and I were so happy. We were told to bring Snappy back to close to where we found him (snapping turtles are territorial and need to stay close to where they came from).

We were so excited to see Snappy. He was in a large plastic container with a lid that had many small holes in it. He had a towel all across the floor of his plastic

Derrian, Ronan, and Tristan help Snappy

242

box. He looked really good - all normal again. Natie said he had made a full recovery and that his eye, his skull, and his front paw were completely healed up. I was so happy for Snappy!

So our next job was to go on Google Maps to try to find a large wild pond or swampy area (back from the road, of course) where we could release him. There were a lot of farmers' fields but no natural ponds or swamps that we could see. Turtles are so much happier in the wild... not stuck in an aquarium. So Snappy was all better and would soon be free again. Derrian, you can tell the rest..."

"Hi! I'm Derrian. I helped Snappy too. We had to bring him back to his home. Tristan remembered which side of the road he was walking to when we found him, after his accident. We all got big boots on and brought our cell phones and a camera. We drove down to Dundalk, where we found him. Daddy drove back and forth until we spotted a farm with a big natural pond away from the road, on the side of the road Snappy was going to.

We stopped and talked to the farmer in front of his house. He said that yes it would be okay to put Snappy in his pond. Nobody swims in there and turtles are good for ponds, he said. He was a nice man. We said thank you!

We helped Daddy lift Snappy's big box out of the minivan. We opened the lid and used the piece of wood Natie said to bring to tip him out of the box. He moved really slowly, looking around, sniffing the air, and we took a lot of photos. He buried his head in some mud and plants by the side of the pond.

Happy Snappy!

243

Thank you to the staff and vets at the Toronto Wildlife Centre (TWC) and for the good advice of TWC director, Nathalie Karvonen. Please contact the Toronto Wildlife Centre if you want to help a sick, injured, or orphaned wild animal in Southern Ontario. http://torontowildlifecentre.com

"This was his home and it was nice and he was happy... Ronan, Tristan, and I said that it was a Happy Snappy Day!"

Did You Know?

- It is very hard to tell the sex of a turtle, oftentimes it requires a vet taking X-rays of the pelvis.

- Common snapping turtles live about 30 years in the wild.

- Snapping turtles are omnivores, eating both plants and animals, and are important aquatic scavengers; but they are also active hunters.

- Snapping turtles prey on anything they can swallow, including many fish, frogs, reptiles (including snakes and smaller turtles), some birds, and small mammals.

Activity Ideas!

- 🐾 Roleplay helping a turtle hit by a car on the road. Think of all the steps to help the turtle.

- 🐾 Research how turtles live and what we as humans can do to stay out of their way and let them thrive in the wild.

- 🐾 Draw an ideal ecosystem in which a turtle might live. Use any medium you wish: digital, painting, etc.

"The most important thing children and teenagers can do to help wildlife is to care about wildlife! If you find a wild animal in distress, get help. Call us for help. Care enough to do something!" Nathalie Karvonen, Director, Toronto Wildlife Centre

Newsflash! Hermit Crabs belong on sandy beaches

Jenny Bain saw a booth at her local mall selling hermit crabs. She knew that hermit crabs live on sandy beaches and that they are very social with each other. She filled out a comment card at the mall, wrote a letter to the mall manager informing the management that she would not shop there until the hermit crab booth was gone. She also said she'd tell her friends and family to not shop until the hermit crab booth was gone. When the time came for the mall manager to renew the booth, the answer was in favor of the hermit crabs. The manager contacted Jenny and let her know her campaign was a success!

Did You Know?

🐾 It is estimated that only 1 in 1,000 sea turtle hatchlings survives to maturity due in large part to human impact in the ocean and on nesting beaches. These impacts can be avoided. HELPING SEA TURTLES SURVIVE STARTS WITH YOU.

🐾 Turtles have lived on this Earth for millions of years.

🐾 Turtles would much rather be free in their natural habitat than live in a glass tank.

🐾 Gopher Tortoises, a relative of turtles can live up to 100 years.

🐾 Turtles don't want to be pets, they want to be free with their own families in their own home.

🐾 Sea Turtle Oversight Protection, Inc. (STOP) was developed out of necessity. STOP is now in its seventh year and has rescued and released over 80,000 sea turtle hatchings.

🐾 The Toronto Wildlife Centre cares for thousands of sick, injured, and orphaned wild animals each year, including many turtles.

🐾 If you see a turtle crossing the road ask a trusted adult to help, and place the turtle on the side of the road the turtle was heading.

🐾 If a captive turtle needs rescuing, contact New York Turtle and Tortoise Society nytts.org to identify the species of turtle and where their natural home is.

Activity Ideas!

❧ STOP ensures municipalities adhere to the coastal lighting ordinances. They work with local municipalities to promote environmental policies that protect sea turtles from lighting. STOP supplies documentation to the local code enforcement officials and works with them to ensure they follow through with enforcement if the property owner is reluctant to change the illegal light fixtures.

❧ Is there a coastal area near you where you can ensure that turtle lighting is safe? Check out details on the STOP web page seaturtleop.org.

❧ The Toronto Wildlife Centre has a very successful Wildlife Hotline to help people help wild animals in distress. Go to the Toronto Wildlife Centre's website at torontowildlifecentre.com and research some ways in which to help wildlife. Then, roleplay a call to the Wildlife Hotline where one person has found a wild animal in distress and the other person is a volunteer from the Toronto Wildlife Centre trying to give good advice to help the animal.

❧ Fishing hooks, nets, and fishing line are a killer of sea life, organize a beach clean-up for wildlife in your area.

247

Chapter 29

Winged Flights to Freedom

Cheers to Sydale for Doing the Right Thing

Sydale was in 5th Grade at Oriole Elementary school. I visited his school and gave out the Animal Hero Cards that are distributed at assembly presentations. Sydale kept his, the card instructs kids on who to call and what to do if you see an animal who needs help.

One week later Sydale was walking to school when he heard a sound coming from behind a bush. He turned to see a mourning dove bleeding from the back of the head as if someone had thrown a rock or something at the little bird. He knew he had to help. Sydale's friends who he was walking to school with said, "who cares, let's go," Sydale said to them, "If I don't help this bird, who will?"

Sydale did the right thing. He remembered my instructions at his school assembly, plus he also had his Animal Hero Card in his pocket. He found

Sydale with Susan and award by wildlife ambulance

a box, put breathing holes in the box before carefully laying the injured bird inside, closing the lid and quietly walked to the school office. The Vice-Principal called the South Florida Wildlife Center ambulance. The bird had to have stitches and then a few weeks later the bird was released back in Sydale's and the dove's neighborhood. The dove flew high in the sky before landing in a nearby tree.

Then I visited Sydale's class and gave him an Animal Hero award. His whole class came outside so we could take a pic in front of the wildlife ambulance.

Sydale told me he wanted to be a chef when he grew up. I arranged with Sydale's mom to meet at Sublime, a vegan gourmet restaurant. Sydale was treated to a tour of the kitchen, and he met all of the chefs there. We enjoyed lunch and spoke of the dove who was flying free and perhaps with her family now, thanks to Sydale's kind actions. We cheered Sydale for doing the right thing.

Class in front of ambulance
http://humaneeducatorsreachingout.com/gallery.htm

Batty about Bats

We met JP in Chapter 10 of Section 1, where he told the story of adopting his special needs dog Bella from a shelter.

JP has another true story about when his family found a bat in a grocery store parking lot, who was obviously weak, and on the ground in dire need of help. Luckily they knew where to take the little bat. Family friends work at the South Florida Wildlife Center in Fort Lauderdale, Florida. The bat was dehydrated, weak, and exhausted. After care, from the center's staff, the day came for the bat to go back to the neighborhood where he was found. Here's JP to tell what happened next...

When we pulled into the Publix parking lot, it was dark and kind of gloomy. But instead of thinking, "This is creepy," I was thinking, "These are perfect flying conditions. For a bat!" I got out of the SUV and ran over to Jennifer and Boyd, our vegan friends who had the little bat in a box. Boyd works at the South Florida Wildlife Center and had nursed the bat back to health.

My step dad found the little bat sitting on the ground in the parking lot in broad daylight and knew something was wrong. He went into the store and got a box, coaxed the bat into the box and got him to Boyd. He said he was lethargic and dehydrated. They had to hand feed him at the center.

And now it was time to release the bat! As soon as I saw him in the box, I felt nervous, as if he were going to attack me. Still I stared at him because my fascination outweighed my fear. I backed up as Boyd started to open the lid of the clear box. Then he picked him up gently with a blue towel, held him up to the night sky, and let him go! I jumped back 3 feet as the bat shot from his hands into a tree! He flew so hard some leaves shook off the tree.

Despite my fear, I felt quite happy that, because of our quick actions, the little bat can live the rest of his life happy and free. It was a very rewarding feeling and I was glad our family and friends could be helpful to animals.

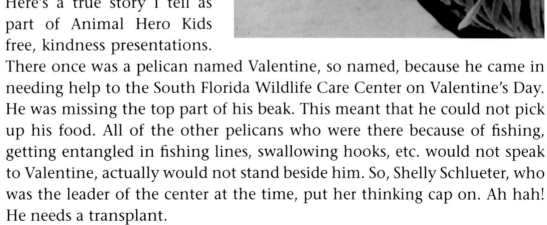

Valentine the Pelican

Here's a true story I tell as part of Animal Hero Kids free, kindness presentations. There once was a pelican named Valentine, so named, because he came in needing help to the South Florida Wildlife Care Center on Valentine's Day. He was missing the top part of his beak. This meant that he could not pick up his food. All of the other pelicans who were there because of fishing, getting entangled in fishing lines, swallowing hooks, etc. would not speak to Valentine, actually would not stand beside him. So, Shelly Schlueter, who was the leader of the center at the time, put her thinking cap on. Ah hah! He needs a transplant.

253

Shelley came up with the idea of asking a dentist who cares about animals to donate some orthodontic wire. Then a beak was taken from a pelican who had died from old age. The new piece of the beak was added to the broken part of Valentine's beak and attached using the waterproof orthodontic materials. All of the volunteers and staff watched as Valentine was put back in with the other pelicans, around the pelican pool, where they rest before their release. The first thing Valentine did was to pick up a fish for the first time since being brought in to the center. He could now feed himself. All of the other pelicans gathered around Valentine speaking in pelican language. In my presentation, I ask the students what they think the other pelicans said to Valentine, some of the answers have been "We're sorry for ignoring you", "How is your beak?, "Will you be my friend?"

Everyone in the class including the adults think about how important it is to accept others' differences when they hear the story of Valentine and his new beak. Valentine turned out to be a perfect name because his story opens hearts.

Did You Know?

* Mourning doves like many birds, including ducks, mate for life.

* Many serious pelican injuries occur due to fishing tackle, balloons, and other plastic items.

* Pelicans are wild animals and need to find their own sources of food to remain independent. Don't feed pelicans!

These two girls, Evan and Nathalie, saw a man shooting wild Quaker parakeets in their neighborhood. Horrified, the girls called the police. The man was charged with animal cruelty. Now the parrots and all the other birds in the neighborhood fly safely thanks to their actions.

255

Chapter 30

Furred Friends in Need

Jasmine, the Defender
You may remember meeting Jasmine in Section 2
in the Fave Vegan Recipe section.

Hi everyone! My name is Jasmine. I am 11 years old. I was just recently nominated as Animal Hero Kids Canada president. My goal is to stop the fur trade in Canada by the time I'm 20. I plan on doing this by sharing truthful information about the fur industry.

What I'm focusing on right now is helping people to see coyotes as the beautiful animals they are, not the way the media makes them sound as ruthless killers. They found a coyote in a snare near where I live. His mouth was torn apart by the snare and he was found near dead. I felt so sad because he suffered like that for days. The town of Pickering has been asked to ban snares and all body-gripping traps. We want to make the trails safe for kids, dogs, cats and the wildlife here. There's a lot to do to make this a fur-free country but we can do it. Every step counts.

When I think of people wearing real fur, I think about my dog being in the trap I'm holding in the photo, how terrified she would be, how a coyote feels that pain, and terror, as she would.

When I think of fur, I imagine myself being in this trap and how I would be terrified, crying for my family, wanting so badly to go home, but can't. Out of desperation I try gnawing at my leg, twisting it, breaking bones, it hurts so much, but no matter how hard I try I cannot break free. I lay down exhausted... and wait to die. If I'm lucky I will die before the trapper shows up. Before he slams me, or chokes me or uses some other terrifying method to kill me before he takes MY skin. Animals trapped for fur, this is their sentence.

When I think of fur it gives me chills knowing people actually wear animals that have been violently killed, and call it fashion. I'm outside all winter in very cold weather for hours and I've never needed fur or down to keep me warm. You don't either.

I think about how we would feel if a much smarter and stronger being came to Earth and did all the things to us we are doing to defenseless animals, and innocent people on our planet.

When I think of fur, I think about how they trick the animals with bait to get them trapped, and then trick the people to think it is ok by covering up the truth, with words like conservation, nuisance control and calling fur green.

You are a victim of the fur industry as much as the animals. You've been lied to, but today I am telling you the truth.

Fur is not cool, it's cruel and it's sad to see people wearing what was once a beautiful animal with a family, a mate, and a love for life. Coyotes are shy, dedicated family members, not the ruthless killers they are made out to be. There has only been one death to a human in 30 years in Canada by a coyote but we have killed hundreds of thousands of them.

I want a fur-free Canada. What do you think? Together, we can make this happen!

You can start by signing my petition asking Dani Reiss of Canada Goose to meet with me to discuss alternatives to using fur and down in jackets. Join Fur-Bearer Defenders and Coyote Watch Canada for more information on the fur industry, coyotes, and the truth behind fur trapping. Speak up for these creatures, they need our voice. Together, our voices will be loud enough to be heard.

Jasmine, Animal Hero Kids Canada president

My name is Jasmine. I'm 11 years old and I know the truth behind fur. Now you do too. What are YOU going to do about it?

Thank you for reading. Please spread the word, don't get caught in the fur trap.

Jasmine wrote this poem:

How would you feel?

How would you feel if a coyote trapped you
bopped you, stomped you, and choked you too
you lay in grim fate, you were tricked by the bait
make you suffer, make you bleed and still full of greed
take your skin even though you would plead.
never will you see your family again
never will you feel the comfort of your den
so next time you think of wearing fur
just ask yourself
how would you feel if a coyote trapped you?

I am glad to take part in protests and vigils where we educate the public on how animals are exploited. My parents respect me enough to listen to me, and raise me knowing I have a voice that can be heard. I have been taught that I can change things I don't think are right like the fur industries that make animals suffer meaninglessly just for fashion, and the circus that abuses animals for someone's pleasure and entertainment. I know I have the power in me to create a world I can live in happily. I think it's an injustice to not listen to your children. I meet a lot of kids who want to be vegan, want to get involved in animal advocacy, environmental and human rights but their parents won't let them. They don't listen to their children, they force their views on them. That's an injustice. I've been taught well enough that I can make choices on what I know to be true. That deserves respect. I don't consider myself forceful with my views. I am kind and considerate but confident enough to speak up.

People my age understand how valuable and precious life is. It is important that we are informed about things like the fur trade because many times kids are told something is ok, and it isn't. Right now, Ontario has approved a trapping program for kids ages 12-16. That is just wrong. They should be teaching people our age how to respect life, not how to take one. The more we know about the world, the more we can help it, and you know what, most kids my age would not want to cause an animal to suffer. When someone asks me what could be so wrong with trapping, I ask them if they would use these devices on their dog or cat. My question is: What is the difference? There is none, they both feel the same pain and suffering. I have written to officials about this program, asking them to instead involve youth in a non-violent program that teaches us to respect and preserve our wilderness. I have received no replies.

The biggest challenge we face is the amount of false information out there, and so many mindless traditions. It can get pretty difficult at times to explain something to someone if they have been taught the opposite all their life. They don't want to accept that they have been lied to all their life, so they would rather think we are the ones lying.

Patrik Ba-boo-me-in is an athlete, who just so happens to be vegan. He was told by so many people that he would never be able to be a heavy weight lifter if he was vegan. He didn't listen to them. Despite what people told him, he did his own research, and wasn't afraid to be different. Patrik set a world record recently for the heaviest weight ever lifted on a yoke. My advice for those who want to be more informed is to not be afraid to ask questions. Don't be afraid to stand up for your views; to not follow the crowd. Join groups that tell you what it's like for the victims such as Fur-Bearer Defenders, and Coyote Watch Canada. They do fantastic work for wildlife and for people with wildlife co-existence programs.

Don't fall for smart advertising that makes kids believe animals aren't hurt for their fur, and don't be afraid to speak up and ask questions like what really happens to the animals. If you are in the Toronto area you can join Fur-Bearer defenders and attend vigils. You can even get your class involved by having events at your school that help raise awareness about the truth behind the cruelty of trapping and wearing fur and faux fur. There are great books about helping animals, you're reading one right now!

Whatever you are concerned about, remember to never give up, always do the best you can! It's so important.

Foxes and Coyotes Saved by Kids Speaking Up

The Fish and Wildlife Commission annual meeting in Lake Mary, Florida was standing room only. The Commission's job is to safeguard wildlife, yet, the commissioners are often also people who like to hunt animals and their salaries are paid from hunting license fees. Can you imagine how hard it would be to speak at a lectern (those stands with a microphone) in a room where there are 250 people, TV cameras, and some stern looking officials?

Animal Hero Kids at Fish and Wildlife Services meeting

I sat waiting for my turn to speak. I was surprised by some very eloquent kids and young teens who spoke, clearly and effectively for foxes and coyotes in crisis. Animal Hero Kids spoke at the Florida Fish and Wildlife Commission's Annual meeting to urge them to ban fox and coyote penning, that's a practice of taking foxes or coyotes and penning them in with fences they can't escape from, and then setting up to 25 or more dogs on them to tear them apart.

A terrible thing that some hunters try to call a sport; I listened to one of the Animal Hero Teens say, "I am an athlete, I'm on my school's swim team and on the basketball team, if fox penning is a sport I'd be ashamed to call myself an athlete." The commissioners listened intently, as a 9 year old girl spoke of the heartbreaking sounds coming from the fox penning business that they moved next door to, and how hunters would just drop off their dogs and the coyotes and foxes would die a slow, terrifying death. She showed the photographs her family had taken of the cruelty. The crowd was quiet as they listened to the children plead to ban fox and coyote penning in the State of Florida.

Then I was surprised, yet again, when the majority of the commissioners agreed to ban fox and coyote penning in Florida. This was a victory, thanks

"If you wouldn't wear your dog ... please don't wear any fur."
—Charlize Theron

in large part, to the family who lived beside a penning operation taking photos, organizing the children, creating a website, and speaking out. I rushed over to the kids and parents during the break and asked if I could take their photo. That's the photo you see on page 264.

Now the family who lived beside the penning operation is taking their fight to end penning nationally, and is working on banning it in the United States. You can read about it at trainingnottorture.org.

A record number of 12 children under the age of 14 spoke that day and saved the lives of countless foxes and coyotes!

Mystery Whistleblower's Action
for Raccoon and Opossum

You read about the whistleblower in Section 2 who saved the piglets who were being abused. There was another whistleblower who was on Facebook and saw a very disturbing video on someone's personal Facebook page showing the person tormenting a raccoon and an opossum who were trapped in a small cage trap.

The whistleblower teen watched the video in horror as the raccoon and opossum died a slow death. The whistleblower sprang into action and copied the video and posted it with the help of a trusted adult on a change. org petition. The petition had the local police stations phone number and e-mail address. Signers were asked to watch the video and then contact local police to ask for felony animal cruelty charges to be laid. Forty eight hours later, there were 30,000 signatures and calls to local officials from as far away as Norway. The person who was laughing as he tortured the caged animals was arrested and charged with felony animal cruelty. The video was taken down by the person who put it on their Facebook page about 30 minutes after putting it up. It would have been lost if it weren't for the whistleblower's quick thinking.

Rocky Raccoon helps with the Stay Wild presentation, which fosters empathy for all creatures and reinforces the need to co-exist peacefully with native wildlife. This is another free program offered by the all-volunteer charity, Animal Hero Kids.

267

Did You Know?

- The term 'whistleblower' was used for the first time in an American newspaper in 1958 and was thought to have come from a policeman blowing a whistle on a crime, or a referee blowing a whistle on a foul ball.

- Every year, in the United States, hunters kill more than 200 million animals. There are twice as many animals being shot as there are people in the whole State of California, (24 million) New York (18 million) Illinois, (11 million), Michigan, (9 million), Ohio, (11 million), Pennsylvania (12 million), and Texas (15 million) put together.

- Many hunters use "calls" that sound like real calls of animals in distress, then blast away when other animals come to the rescue.

- Only 7% of Americans hunt. Some hunters say if they don't kill animals in the fall, they'll starve in the winter, yet the animals were on the earth long before humans and were fine.

P!nk says, "I've always felt that animals are the purest spirits in the world. They don't fake or hide their feelings, and they are the most loyal creatures on Earth and somehow we humans think we're smarter—what a joke."

No fur coats allowed.
_Pink

Activity Ideas!

❧ If you live out in the countryside, make big signs that say "No Hunting" and hang them on trees and fences all over your property.

❧ Some plots of land have been saved for animals. These are called wildlife refuges. Refuge means a safe shelter from danger, however, some refuges allow people to hunt on them. Write to your congressperson to ask them to not allow hunting on areas that are supposed to be safe zones. An Internet search will tell you who your congressperson, senator, or member of parliament is.

❧ Consider forming an Animal Hero Kids crew in your community.

❧ Helpinganimals.com has a PETA fact sheet called "Why Sport Hunting is Cruel and Unnecessary."

❧ Create your own poem or song about how wearing fur is mean and cruel.

❧ If you need help with a protest or with organizing a project or any other act relating to helping animals, please e-mail: education@animalherokids.org.

❧ One last thing, please re-use this book, donate it to a library, a school, or community group. Contact education@animalherokids. org to ask about our free, humane education programs, and free Be an Animal Hero Kits for schools.

❧ Be a hero through acts of kindness and compassion! Speak up for those who can't help themselves... you could be their only voice.

Winners of the "Be Kind to All Animals" Poster Contest

Create your own animal hero poster and scan and send it to education@ animalherokids.org and you may see it on our website!

Appendix

Did You Know? Animal Hero Kids Glossary

Animal Hero Kid/Teen: any young person who helps animals in need

Animal Hero Kids Role Model: someone who exemplifies compassion-to-animal qualities to aspire to

Community Cats: cats who live outside in a maintained cat colony who receive vaccinations and are spayed/neutered and monitored by a cat caregiver

Factory Farming: intensive farming of animals in which they are denied fresh air, space, and access to their young

Kind2all: an Animal Hero Kids award for someone who helps all species of animals, Example: 1. companion animals, by spaying and neutering companion animals, and adopting; 2. farmed animals, by not eating them; 3. wild animals, by not going to see shows that exploit wildlife.

Returning Hero Award: someone who returned after hardship and challenges to their home; this award has been given to cats and dogs so far

TNR: Trap Neuter and Return, the practice of spaying and neutering community cats

Vegan: someone who eats no animals or products taken from animals, including dairy and eggs, sometimes to reduce animal cruelty, or for the environment, or to benefit their own health. Vegan shoes/sandals/boots, purses, belts, and other accessories (i.e., not made from animal products such as leather/suede) are popular with vegans.

Vegetarian: someone who does not eat animals, including fish

Whistleblower: a person who informs on a person or organization engaged in an illegal or unethical activity

About the Author

My first realization that we shared the planet with magical beings came early. Other beings communicated to me in a wide variety of ways, with their own distinct form of language. At three years old, I have a crisp memory of meeting a white duck. I crouched down to the duck's eye level, face to beak. I saw calm intelligence looking back steadily at me.

Thanks to my grandfather, Joseph Tyrrell, from Ballinasloe, County Galway, Ireland, I met many winged and furred, creatures. He cared for all of the animals in need in our little English town of St. Helens, just outside of Liverpool. All manner of birds with hurt wings, in shock, and abandoned pets. I loved going to the whitewashed brick house where there was always any number of species in various stages of being nursed back to health.

My grandfather had a strong sense of justice, he did not tolerate bullies, and cared deeply for the underdog, whether they happened to be human or non-human. He admired Michael Collins, the great Irish freedom fighter. My grandfather described to me, in flowing detail, scenes of rabbits leaping and dancing on mid-summer's eve in green forests. I believed him, wholeheartedly. Picturing the Irish fairies welcoming the rabbits with nectar held aloft in bluebell flower cups. Years later, caring for displaced rabbits who were abandoned after being bought in pet stores, I saw bunny ballet first hand. Rabbits will leap and pirouette in the air with great speed and grace, when happy, as long as there is space.

At nine years old, I was taken to a chicken hatchery and saw all of the male chicks being gassed and suffocated. I was shocked to discover the mass killing of non-laying chickens after hatching on conveyor belts is standard industry practice. When I was thirteen, I organized a Toronto school walk-out in protest of the Canadian seal slaughter. I became determined to help the beleaguered and voiceless creatures with whom we are sharing this Earth.

I have been a volunteer, wildlife rehabilitator and releaser, a direct action animal activist, a creative protest organizer (the first real We'd Rather Go Naked Than Wear Fur protest), a non-violent civil disobedience participant, an undercover investigator, an animal rights radio show host, an under-the-radar rescuer, a hunt saboteur, an unwelcome surprise guest on fur show runways... and, most of my life, a humane educator.

Animal Hero Kids

It has been my privilege to meet many heroes along the way... heroes of all ages, heroes who are two legged or, in some cases, four legged. It is these heroes, who may brave ridicule, danger, or grave distress to do the right thing you can discover in this book. These beings who go above and beyond to help others. Their stories fuel my determination to continue the fight for other animals to live free of harm, a determination my grandfather fostered in me over five decades ago.

For the animals and the planet,
Susan Hargreaves
animalherokids.org

Susan Hargreaves with Winnie, the 8 month old three-legged puppy rescued from certain death by kind and courageous Animal Hero Kids. (story on page 14)

Acknowledgements

Thank you to Rebecca for supporting my need to shed light on the untold suffering of other animals. Our family, two legged and four, is home.

Thanks to Mum for reminding me, consistently, to write, as only a mum can, like "I just saw a book about kids helping animals and it was not written by you" and other such gems. Thanks, Mum, for your heartfelt encouragement.

Dad has always been a great example of how to enjoy life, from a very young age I saw his joy, and his sense of humor.

Thank you to Ronald Nistico-Palamara for his unerring support for this book, and for our 30 year friendship.

Tanjah Karvonen helped accomplish the unthinkable: organizing me on a timeline I succeeded in sticking to, most of the time. Tanjah's editorial and organizational talents are considerable.

Cynthia Cake's creative design combined with her attention to detail have crafted a beautiful book.

Thank you Elizabeth Rhodes, a lifetime animal hero, who has painted banners and attended protests and supported animal rights well into her 90's.

Ken with Linda Brown Charities can always be trusted to be pragmatic, direct, and supportive.

Thank you Rudy for seeing the potential in the idea of Animal Hero Kids.

Thanks to Lizzie Lerer of dodo.com for her generosity in allowing Animal Hero Kids to use her stories.

Joseph Connelly and Chas Chiodo, thank you for wonderful support.

Thank you Brenda Bronfman for headquartering Animal Hero Kids Canada at her Wishing Well Sanctuary.

Ingrid Newkirk is a wealth of inspiration and is always willing to help sincere folks who want to help all animals.

Daniel Crowe, the talented Animal Hero Kids web designer is a genuine gem.

Thanks to M and M Studios for their assistance with creating top notch awards.

Frank Balzano and Linda Weeks from the Art Institute of Fort Lauderdale and Gary Lavasser and Jack Keebler from the Art Institute of Los Angeles have repeatedly donated their artistic skill and their students' time.

Dave and Carol Keyworth, thank you for helping with reviewing and feedback.

Photo Credits

Cover: Katie and Colby Procyk; Dedication: The Catherine Violet Hubbard Foundation and teach-kind.org

Section 1: Dominic and Luna: Tina Valant

Arielle: Alexi Howk

Aailiyana: Maria Falconi

p. 3 Marco Morales, Art Institute of Los Angeles, Ellen Award design.

p. 6 Heather Hyde

p. 7 Michele Cintron

p. 8 Photo Voice

p. 9 Tina Valant

p. 13 Leslie Walters, Artworks

p. 14 Ricky Williams photo, Patti Roth

p. 18 Patti Roth

p. 19 Miami Herald with permission

p. 23 Ken in the Philipines

p. 28 Lovey, Tina Valant

p. 30 Kit Bradshaw with permission

p. 34 Katie and Colby Procyck

p. 38 Lou Wegner

p. 41 Heather Hyde

p. 44 Hugo rescue

p. 46 Tina Valant

p. 47 Leslie Walters, Artworks

p. 48 Cristina Blancard

p. 50 Jacob Richter

p. 52 Tina Valant

p. 56 Dave Robertson

p. 59 Dave Robertson

p. 62 Jennifer Cohen

p. 66 John Steed

p. 69 the Ellen (DeGeneres) Show

p. 70 Monica K. Reeve

Pp. 76-77 "Be Kind to All Animals" Poster Contest Winners

Section 2: p. 78 Zach Teper

p. 80 Keenie Valega, cow image, Art Institute student

p. 81 PETA

p. 86 animalherokids.org Val Silidiker

p. 88 Dora Falconi

p. 90 Maria Falconi

p. 91 Veganism Worldwide

p. 92 Courtesy of NPR

p. 95 Heather Hyde

p. 96 Pelican Harbor

p. 98 Duchess Sanctuary A. Gritta

p. 101 Panhandle Equine Rescue

p. 104 AnimalHeroKids.org

p. 106 Agnes Cseke

p. 107 Brenda Bronfman

p. 108 Kelli Polsinelli

p. 109 PIGS Animal Sanctuary

p. 110 Kevin Storm

p. 115 Peace Abbey, Rand Family

p. 117 W. Hillman

p. 125 Full Circle Farm Sanctuary

p. 124 Edgars Mission

p. 126 animalherokids.org

p. 128 Heather Hyde

p. 129 Rooterville Pig Sanctuary

p. 130 Animalherokids.org

p. 131 AnimalHeroKids.org

p. 132 AnimalHeroKids.org

p. 135 film posters

p. 136 Gentle Barn

Saoirse, the Super Animal Hero

Saoirse is a magical, super animal hero who lives deep in the Florida Everglades.

Her home's entrance is hidden by banyan tree roots and a curtain of spanish moss. Saoirse has wings, which turn into fins under water and can fold into her shoulder blades when they need to be hidden. Saoirse is pronounced "Sear-shaw" which means "freedom" in Irish. She and her best friend Tunika, fight animal cruelty wherever it exists.

Tunika volunteers at Animal Voices United, a rescue shelter for injured and orphaned wildlife and displaced domestic animals. Some of the rescued animals are: cats, chickens, dogs, rabbits and cows.

Saoirse's ties her long red hair with Spanish moss. When she was a child, she wore glasses, and still does at times, but now they're shaped like hawk wings. At school, she was teased for having red hair and for wearing glasses. When she wears them Saoirse can see as keenly as a hawk.

Saoirse's friends deep in the everglades include Florida panthers, alligators, opossums, ospreys and great blue herons. These neighbors have their own ethical code, methods of communication and sense of community; a true "Animal Nation."

Saoirse communicates with the Animal Nation with important news or if a disaster strikes. To listen she lays her ear along the base of a tree root; to speak, she gently whispers into the wind. The Nation recently sent this message: "Fire in South Florida has destroyed many Animal homes. There's an urgent need for shelter and food for squirrels, rabbits and tortoises. Please donate food at the top of your tallest tree. Saoirse, the brave one, is leading hundreds of flocks of pelicans to quench the flames. Saoirse knows who set the fire. It won't happen again!"

Saoirse can hear heartfelt calls for help for all non-human animals. Here's how she met Tunika:

One morning as Saoirse sat in her Spanish moss covered chair looking up through the banyan branches, she heard an echoing call of distress; a heartfelt plea. She sprung to her feet and soared upward through the treetops, following the calls for help.

She saw a group of bullies tormenting a black homeless cat, and a young girl trying to protect her. The gang thought it was "cool" to hurt this helpless being. Tunika cried out against this cruelty, with lightning speed Saoirse landed, her feet planted firmly on the ground.

Saoirse has the power to stop all movement and she immediately froze the harmful acts. As the bullies awoke they found themselves inside the body of the cat. They could now feel her fear as their own, "You will feel her terror as your terror. You will feel her fear and sadness as yours, and you will each be changed forever!" Through this, Saoirse empowered the bullies with a true sense of empathy and love for all beings.

Saoirse praised Tunika's courage for standing up for the cat who was in danger.

"I volunteer at Animal Voices United sanctuary where I nurse creatures in crisis," Tunika told her. I started a "justice for animals club" at my school. We cook and bake great cruelty-free vegan food for the school cafeteria."

Saoirse is impressed by this young dynamo. "Sometimes I need a clear voice to get the message out about co-existing with wildlife and the vital importance of being kind, strong and brave. Will you be that voice, Tunika?"

"Absolutely!" Tunika replied.

The bullies who tried to harm the black cat now volunteer at Animal Voices United. They alert the community about free spay and neuter services for dogs and cats, and educate schools about the homeless cat and dog epidemic. Their new band, "Power Kind" plays at concerts to raise money for the sanctuary. Tunika is their songwriter.

Saoirse is back in her Everglades home looking out her camouflaged window at the mother opossum sleeping soundly on the widest part of a branch. Her babies are peaceful and still inside her pouch. Saoirse lies down on her Spanish moss bower and closes her eyes, secure in her knowledge that crow sentries will alert her to any danger. She rests to be ready for the next crisis call she will certainly hear.

Saoirse will eventually save the earth and the animal nation with her amazing ability to make humans feel and experience the emotions and suffering of abused animals. This empathetic conscience is not temporary, it is long term and inspires the changed person to speak out on behalf of others. They become aware of the effect their actions have on the planet and on the other animals they share it with.

Animal Hero Kids

Voices for the Voiceless

Book a free humane education program

- Participate
- Educate
- Nominate
- Donate

AnimalHeroKids.org

ANIMAL HERO CARD

ANIMAL HERO KIDS
ACTION CARD

I_____

pledge to be kind to the other animals
and to the earth.
I will never harm an animal.
I promise to help any animal in danger.
I realize that wild animals need to stay with
their families in their natural homes.
I will be kind to this earth by recycling,
and never littering.
I will never ignore an animal in need.
I will be part of the solution for homeless
animals and promise to adopt not shop.
I will not attend rodeos, circuses, or
aquarium shows where animals
are abused for profit.
I promise to advocate for the spay and
neuter of companion animals.
I will be a voice for the voiceless by
speaking out against cruelty.